I0828648

A COMPILATION

OF

PENSION, PAY

AND

BOUNTY LAWS:

TOGETHER WITH

FULL INSTRUCTIONS, FORMS AND DECISIONS, RELATIVE TO PRESENTING GOVERNMENT CLAIMS.

LAWS, By SNYDER, COOK & Co.
INSTRUCTIONS, Etc., By LEAVITT & WRIGHT,

ATTORNEYS-AT-LAW, CHICAGO, ILLINOIS.

CHICAGO:
PUBLISHED BY THE TRIBUNE COMPANY, 51 CLARK STREET.
1862.

PENSION and BOUNTY BLANKS of every description kept constantly on hand at TRIBUNE Office.

PUTNAM'S

MAMMOTH EASTERN

CLOTHING EMPORIUM

LEADER OF FASHIONS & REGULATOR OF PRICES !

The Crowds who daily make their purchase at this Establishment, is a sure evidence that we are selling the Best Made Fashionable Garments

TWENTY PER CENT. LESS

Than can be Bought elsewhere in the city.

AN EXAMINATION OF OUR STOCK AND PRICES

WILL CONVINCE YOU OF THE FACT.

Everybody goes to Putnam's, the Leading Institution of Chicago,

116 & 118 RANDOLPH STREET.

A COMPILATION

OF

PENSION, PAY

AND

BOUNTY LAWS:

TOGETHER WITH

FULL INSTRUCTIONS, FORMS AND DECISIONS, RELATIVE TO PRESENTING GOVERNMENT CLAIMS.

LAWS, By SNYDER, COOK & Co.

INSTRUCTIONS, Etc., By LEAVITT & WRIGHT,

ATTORNEYS-AT-LAW, CHICAGO, ILLINOIS.

CHICAGO:

PUBLISHED BY THE TRIBUNE COMPANY, 51 CLARK STREET.

1862.

PUBLISHERS' NOTICE.

The following compilation of Laws, together with the Forms, Instructions, and Decisions, is intended as a cheap, convenient and practical guide in the prosecution of claims against the Government arising out of the present war. It comprises all the laws now in force relating to Pensions, Pay of the Army, and Bounty Money, official decisions and opinions thereon, and instructions as to the proper form in which claims should be presented. It also contains a full and complete set of plain and simple Forms, with numerous explanatory notes for filling them up. These Forms are constantly used with success by the compilers of this work, and have been approved by the Departments; and many of them are to be found in no other work. Many new rules and regulations have been adopted by the Government in regard to this kind of claims, which are here, for the first time, collected and published. The Laws have been compiled by Messrs. Snyder, Cook & Co., Attorneys, and the Appendix, including the Instructions, Forms and Official Opinions and Decisions, is by Messrs. Leavitt & Wright, Attorneys. These gentlemen are engaged in procuring War Claims in this city, and have sufficiently attested their accuracy and value in their daily practice.

TRIBUNE CO.

Entered according to Act of Congress, in the year 1862,
BY SNYDER, COOK & CO.,
In the Clerk's Office of the District Court for the Northern District of Illinois.

CONTENTS.

CONTENTS.

A COMPILATION

OF

PENSION, PAY AND BOUNTY LAWS.

CHAPTER I.

OF PENSIONS AND HALF PAY FOR MILITARY SERVICES.

ACT OF MARCH 16, 1802.

SEC. 14. *And be it further enacted*, That if any officer, non-commissioned officer, musician, or private, in the corps composing the peace establishment of the United States, shall be disabled by wounds or otherwise, while in the line of his duty in public service, he shall be placed on the list of invalids of the United States, at such rate of pay, and under such regulations as may be directed by the President, for the time being; *Provided always*, That the compensation to be allowed for such wounds or disabilities to a commissioned officer, shall not exceed for the highest rate of disability, half the monthly pay of such officer at the time of his being disabled or wounded; and no officer shall receive more than the half pay of a lieutenant-colonel; and the rate of compensation to non-commissioned officers, musicians and privates, shall not exceed five dollars per month; *And Provided, also*, That all inferior disabilities shall entitle the person so disabled to receive an allowance proportionate to the highest disability.

Pensions allowed to wounded soldiers.

Provided, the compensation shall not exceed half the monthly pay.

Rate to privates not to exceed $5 per month.

Allowances for inferior disabilities to be in proportion.

SEC. 15. *And be it further enacted*, That if any commissioned officer in the military peace establishment of the United States shall, while in the service of the United States, die, by reason of any wound received in actual service of the United States, and leave a widow, or if no widow, a child or children under sixteen years of age, such widow, or if no widow, such child or children, shall be entitled to and receive half the monthly pay, to which the deceased was entitled at the time of his death, for and during the term of five years. But in

Pensions allowed widows and children of those who die or are killed in service.

Pension to close on death or intermarriage of such widow.

the case of the death or intermarriage of such widow, before the expiration of the said five years, the half pay, for the remainder of the time, shall go to the child or children of

Proviso.

such deceased officer; *Provided always*, That such half pay shall cease, on the decease of such child or children.

ACT OF AUGUST 2, 1813.

Widow and children under 16 years of those who die in the service entitled to pension.

SECTION 1. If any commissioned officer of the militia, or of any volunteer corps shall, while in the service of the United States, die by reason of any wound received in the actual service of the United States, and leave a widow, or if no widow, a child or children under sixteen years of age, such widow, or if no widow, such child or children, shall be entitled to receive half the monthly pay to which the deceased was entitled at the time of his death, for and during the term of five years; but in the case of the death or intermarriage of such widow, before the expiration of the said term of five years, the half pay for the remainder of the time, shall go to

Proviso.

the child or children of such deceased officer; *Provided always*, That such half pay shall cease on the death of such child or children.

Pensions allowed to wounded and disabled soldiers.

SEC. 2. If any officer, non-commissioned officer, musician, or private of the militia, or of any volunteer corps, shall be disabled by known wounds received in the actual service of the United States, while in the line of his duty, he shall, upon substantiating his claim, in the manner described by an act, entitled, "An act to provide for persons who were disabled by known wounds received in the revolutionary war," passed the tenth day of April, eighteen hundred and six, be placed on the list of invalids of the United States, at such rate of pension, and under such regulations as are provided by the

Provided the compensation shall not exceed half the monthly pay.

said act, or as may hereafter be provided by law; *Provided always*, That the compensation to be allowed for such wounds or disabilities, to a commissioned officer, shall not exceed for

Rate to non-commissioned officers and privates not to exceed $5 per month.

the highest rate of disability, half the monthly pay of such officer at the time of his being wounded or disabled, and that no officer shall receive more than the half pay of a lieutenant-colonel; and that the rate of compensation to non-commissioned officers, musicians and privates, shall not exceed five dollars per month; *And provided also*, That all inferior disabilities shall entitle the persons so disabled, to receive an allowance proportionate to the highest disability. Inferior disabilities to be paid in proportion.

ACT OF JANUARY 29, 1813.

SECTION 1. If any officer of the navy, or marines, shall be killed, or die by reason of a wound received in the line of his duty, leaving a widow, or if no widow, a child, or children, under sixteen years of age, such widow, or if no widow, such child, or children, shall be entitled to receive half the monthly pay to which the deceased was entitled at the time of his death; which allowance shall continue for and during the term of five years; but in the case of the death or intermarriage of such widow, before the expiration of the said term of five years, the half-pay for the remainder of the time shall go to the child, or children of said deceased officer; *Provided*, That such half-pay shall cease on the death of such child, or children, and the money required for this purpose shall be paid out of the Navy Pension Fund, under the directions of the Commissioners of that Fund. Pension to widow or children.

SEC. 10. *And be it further enacted*, That if any officer, non-commissioned officer, private or musician, shall be disabled by wounds or otherwise, while in the line of his duty in public service, he shall be placed on the lists of invalids of the United States at such rate of pension and under such regulation as may be by law, or are by law directed; *Provided always*, That the compensation to be allowed for such wounds or disabilities to a commissioned officer, shall not exceed for the highest rate of disability half the monthly pay of such officer at the time of his being disabled or wounded; and that no officer shall receive more than the half pay of a lieutenant-colonel; and that the rate of compensation to non-commissioned officers, privates and musicians, shall not exceed $5 per month. Pension not to exceed half pay.

And provided also, That all inferior disabilities shall entitle the person so disabled to receive an allowance proportionate to the highest disability.

SEC. 11. Makes provision in case of death of soldier, etc., for the widow or children, for five years, drawing same.

ACT OF APRIL 16, 1816.

Term of enlistment.

SECTION 1. When any officer or private soldier of the militia, including rangers, sea fencibles and volunteers, or any non-commissioned officer, musician or private, enlisted for either the terms of one year or eighteen months, or any commissioned officer of the regular army, shall have died while in the service of the United States, during the late war (1812,) or in returning to place of residence, after being mustered out of service, or who shall have died at any time thereafter, in consequence of wounds received whilst in the service, and shall have left a widow, or if no widow, a child or children under sixteen years of age, such widow, or if no widow, such child or children, shall be entitled to receive half the monthly pay to which the deceased was entitled at the time of his death, for and during the term of five years; and in case of death or intermarriage of such widow before the expiration of said five years, the half pay for the remainder of the time shall go to the child or children of said decedent; *Provided always*, That the Secretary of War shall adopt such forms of evidence under this act as the President may prescribe; *Provided also*, That the officers and private soldiers of the militia, as aforesaid, who have been disabled by wounds or otherwise, while in the service of the United States in the discharge of their duty, during the late war, shall be placed on the list of pensioners, in the same manner as the officers and soldiers of the regular army, under such forms of evidence as the President of the United States may prescribe; *Provided also*, That the provisions of this act shall not extend to any person embraced in the provision of an act, entitled, "An Act to provide for the widows and orphans of militia slain, and for militia disabled, in the service of the United States," passed August 2nd, 1813.

What heirs entitled.

Half pay.

Half pay in certain cases goes to children.

Wounded Militia on same footing with regular army.

This act not to extend to those provided for by act 1813.

ACT OF JULY 4th, 1836.

Granting half pay to widows or orphans, where their husbands or fathers have died of wounds received in the military service of the United States, in certain cases, and for other purposes.

Be it enacted by the Senate and House of Representatives of the United States of America, in Congress assembled, That any officer, non-commissioned officer, musician, or private of the militia, including rangers, sea-fencibles, and volunteers, who shall have died while in the service of the United States, since the twentieth of April, eighteen hundred and eighteen, or who shall have died in consequence of a wound received whilst in the service, since the day aforesaid, and shall have left a widow, or, if no widow, a child, or children under sixteen years of age, such widow, or, if no widow, such child, or children, shall be entitled to receive half the monthly pay to which the deceased was entitled at the time of his death, or receiving such wound, for and during the term of five years; and in case of the death or marriage of said widow before the expiration of said five years, the half pay for the remainder of the time shall go to the children of the said decedent; *Provided*, That the half pay aforesaid shall be the half monthly pay of the officers, non-commissioned officers, musicians, and privates of the infantry of the regular army, and no more; *Provided, also*, That no greater sum shall be allowed to the widow, or the child or children, of any officer than the half pay of a lieutenant-colonel.

Widows, and children under 16 years, of those who die or are killed in the service, to be entitled to half pay pensions for 5 years.

Pensions to go to children if widow marries.

Half pay to be that of regular army.

No greater allowance than half pay of a Lieut.-Colonel.

SEC. 2. *And be it further enacted*, That if any officer, non-commissioned officer, musician, soldier, Indian spy, mariner or marine, whose service during the Revolutionary War, was such as is specified in the act passed the seventh of June, eighteen hundred and thirty-two, entitled "An act supplementary to the act for the relief of certain surviving officers and soldiers of the Revolution," have died since the 4th of March, eighteen hundred and thirty-one, and before the date of said act, the amount of pension that would have accrued from the fourth of March eighteen hundred and thirty-one, to the time of his death and become payable to him by virtue of that act, if he had survived the passage thereof, shall be paid to his widow; and if he left no widow, to his children, in the manner prescribed in the act hereby amended.

Pensions which have accrued since 4th of March 1831, to be paid to widow and children in certain cases.

SEC. 3. *And be it further enacted*, That if any person who served in the war of the Revolution, in the manner specified in the act passed the seventh day of June, eighteen hundred and thirty-two, entitled "An act supplementary to the act for the relief of certain surviving officers and soldiers of the Revolution," have died, leaving a widow, whose marriage took place before the expiration of the last period of his service, such widow shall be entitled to receive during

Widow to receive the pension which might have been allowed her husband, during the time she remained unmarried.

the time she may remain unmarried, the annuity or pension which might have been allowed to her husband, by virtue of the act aforesaid, if living at the time it was passed.

No sale, or mortgage of claim to be of any effect.

SEC. 4. *And be it further enacted*, That any pledge, mortgage, sale, assignment or transfer of any right, claim, or interest in any money or half pay granted by this act, shall be utterly void and of no effect: each person acting for, and in behalf of, any one entitled to money under this act, shall take and subscribe an oath, to be administered by the proper accounting officer, and retained by him, put on file, before a warrant shall be delivered to him, that he has no interest in said money by any pledge, mortgage, sale, assignment, or tranfer, and that he does not know or believe that the same has been so disposed of to any person whatever.

Oath to be taken that party has no interest.

Forms of evidence.

SEC. 5. *And be it further enacted*, That the Secretary of War shall adopt such forms of evidence, in application under this act, as the President of the United States may prescribe.

[APPROVED July 4, 1836.]

ACT OF MARCH 3, 1815,

Three months pay.

SEC. 6. Makes provision for paying each commissioned officer who becomes deranged by virtue of this act three months pay at the time of his discharge.

SEC. 7. Officers, non-commissioned officers, musicians and privates shall be entitled to the same provisions for wounds and disabilities, the same provisions for widows and children and the same benefits and all the allowances in every respect, not inconsistent with the provisions of this Act, as are authorized by Act of March 16, 1802, and of Act of April 12, 1808.

ACT OF AUGUST 2, 1813.

Authorizes the Secretary of the Navy to put persons who have been wounded or disabled on board of private armed vessels on the pension list.

ACT OF APRIL 10, 1806.

Revolutionary War Pension.

SECTION 1. *Be it enacted*, That if any commissioned or non-commissioned officer, marine, soldier, mariner or seaman who may be disabled while in the actual service of the United States, while in the line of his duty, by known wounds received while in the revolutionary war, and who did not desert its service; or who in consequence of disability as aforesaid, was taken captive by the enemy, and remained either in captivity or on parole, until the close of said revolutionary war, or who, in consequence of known wounds received as aforesaid, has, at any period since, become and continued disabled in such manner as to render him unable to procure a subsistence by manual labor, whether such officer, mariner, soldier, marine or seaman, served as a volunteer in any proper service against the common enemy, or belonged to a detachment of the militia which served against the common enemy, or to the regular forces of the United States, or of any particular State, he shall, upon substantiating his claim in the manner hereinafter described, be placed on the pension list of the United States, during life, or the continuance of such disability, and be entitled, under the regulations hereinafter mentioned, to receive such sum as shall be found just and proper by the testimony adduced.

How long pension continues.

SEC. 2. In substantiating such claim, the following rules and regulations shall be complied with, that is to say:

All evidence shall be taken on oath or affirmation, before the judge of the district or one of the judges of the Territory in which such claimant resides, or before some person especially authorized by commission before said judge.

How disability proven.

Decisive disability, the effect of known wounds received while in the actual service or line of duty, against the common enemy during the revolutionary war, must be proved by the affidavit of the commanding officer of the regiment, corps, company, ship, vessel, or craft, in which such complainant served; or of two creditable witnesses to the same effect, setting forth the time when, and the place where such known wound or wounds were received, and particularly describing the same. The nature of such disability and in what degree it prevents the claimant from obtaining his subsistence, must be proved by the affidavit of some respectable physician or surgeon, stating his opinion, either from his own knowledge and acquaintance with the claimant, or from an examination of such claimant, on oath or affirmation; which will be necessary for that purpose, shall be administered to such claimant by said judge or commissioner. And the said physician or surgeon, in his affidavit, shall particularly describe the wound or wounds from whence the disability appears to be derived.

Evidence required.

Every claimant must prove, by at least one credible witness, that he continued in service during the whole time for which he was detached, or for which he engaged, unless he was discharged, or left the service in consequence of some derangement of the army, or in consequence of his disability resigned his commission, or was after his disability in captivity, or on parole until the close of the revolutionary war. And in the same manner must prove his mode of life and employment since he left the service, and the place or places where he has since resided, and his place of residence at the time of taking such testimony.

Affidavit required.

Every claimant shall, by his affidavit, give satisfactory reasons why he did not make application for a pension before, and that he is not on the pension list of any State; and the judge or commissioner shall certify, in writing, his opinion of the credibility of the witnesses whose affidavits he shall take, in all those cases where by this act it is said that the proof shall be made by a credible witness or witnesses; and also, that the examining physician or surgeon is respectable in his profession.

When pension to commence.

SEC. 4. Every pension or income thereof by virtue of this act, shall commence on the day when the claimant shall have completed his testimony before the authority proper to take the same.

When pension increased.

SEC. 5. An increase of pension may be allowed to persons already placed upon the pension list of the United States, for disabilities caused by known wounds received during the revolutionary war, in all cases where justice shall require the same; *Provided*, That the increase when added to the pension formerly received shall in no case exceed a full pension.

Full Pension.

SEC. 6. A full pension given by this act to a commissioned officer, shall be one-half of the monthly pay, legally allowed at the time of incurring said disability, to his grade in the forces raised by the United States; and the proportions less than a full pension, shall be the correspondant proportions of said half pay; and a full pension to a non-commissioned officer, musician, soldier, marine, or seaman, shall be five dollars per month, and the proportions less than a full pension, shall be the like proportions of five dollars a month; but no pension of a commissioned officer shall be calculated at a higher rate than the half pay of a lieutenant-colonel.

SEC. 7. The pensions, or increase thereof which may be allowed by this act, shall be paid in the same manner as pensions to individuals who have been heretofore placed on the pension list, are now paid, and under such restrictions and regulations, in all respects, as are prescribed by law.

Transfer of Pension invalid.

SEC. 8. No sale, transfer, or mortgage, of the whole or any part of the pension payable to any non-commissioned officer, musician, soldier, marine or seaman, before the same becomes due, shall be valid. And every person claiming such pension or any part thereof, under power of attorney or substitution, shall, before the same is paid, make oath or affirmation, before some magistrate, legally authorized to take the same, a copy, of which, attested by some magistrate, shall be lodged with the person who pays said pension, that such power or substitution is not given by reason of any transfer of such pension or any part thereof. And any person who shall swear or affirm falsely in the premises, and be thereof convicted, shall suffer as for willful and corrupt perjury.

Prior Laws repealed.

SEC. 9. All laws of the United States heretofore passed, so far as they authorize persons to be placed on the pension list of the United States, for and in consequence of disabilities derived from known wounds received in the revolutionary war, shall be, and they are hereby repealed; *Provided*, That nothing in this repealing clause shall injure, or in any way effect, those persons already upon the pension lists of the United States; and that the Secretary for the War Department shall proceed upon the testimony which has been transmitted to him by any claimant before the passage of this act, in the same manner as though this act had never been passed.

Limitation.

SEC. 10. This act, so far as it authorizes the admission of persons upon the pension list of the United States, shall remain in force for and during the space of six years from the passage thereof, and no longer; *Provided*, That this limitation shall not effect or impair the right of any individual who may have completed his testimony, in the manner prescribed by this act, before this limitation commences its operation, but which has not been transmitted to the Secretary for the Department of War.

PENSION OFFICE, July 9, 1836.

In order to carry into effect the act of Congress of July, 1836, entitled "An act granting half pay to the widows or orphans where their husbands and fathers have died of wounds received in the military service of the United States, in certain cases and for other purposes," the following rules have been prescribed by the President of the United States, and adopted by the Secretary of War, and they are now published for the information of applicants under that law:

1. Applicants under the first section of the act must produce the best proof the nature of the case will allow as to the service of the deceased officer or soldier, the time when he died, and the complaint of which he died, and the supposed cause of his decease.

It must be clearly shown in what company and regiment, or corps, he served, and the grade he held.

Such proof must be had either from the records of the War Department, the muster rolls, the testimony of commissioned officers, or the affidavits of persons of known respectability.

From similar sources evidence must be derived as to the period and cause of death of the officer or soldier.

2. The legality of the marriage, the name of the widow, with those of her children who may have been under sixteen years of age at the time of the father's decease, with the State or Territory and county in which she and they reside, should be established.

The legality of the marriage may be ascertained by the certificate of the clergyman who joined them in wedlock, or the testimony of respectable persons having knowledge of the fact.

The age and number of children may be ascertained by the deposition of the mother, accompanied by the testimony of respectable persons having knowledge of them, or by transcripts from the parish registers, duly authenticated.

The widow, at the time of allowing the half pay or placing her on the list for it, must show that she has not again married; and must, moreover, repeat this at the time of receiving each and every payment thereof: because in case of her marrying again, the half pay to her ceases, and the half pay for the remainder of the time shall go to the child or children of the decedent. This may be done by the affidavits of respectable persons having knowledge of the case.

3. In cases where there are children, and no widow, their guardian will, of course, act for them, and establish their claims as prescribed in the foregoing regulations, and receive their stipends for them.

4. Applicants under the second section of the law will make a declaration before a court of record, setting forth, according to the best of her (or their) knowledge or belief, the names and rank of the field and company officers, the day (if possible) and the month, and year when the claimants' husband or father (as the case may be) entered the service, and the time when he left the same, and, if under more than one engagement, the claimants must specify the particular periods, and the ranks and names of the officers under whom the service was performed; the town or county and State in which the claimants' husband or father resided when he entered the service: whether he was drafted or volunteered, or was a substitute; the battles, if any, in which he was engaged; the country through which he marched; with such further particulars as may be useful in the investigation of the claim; and, also, if the fact be so, that the claimant has no documentary evidence in support of the claim.

5. The same description of proof as to the relationship of the claimant to the deceased officer or soldier will be required as the rule under the first section points out.

6. Claimants under the third section of the law must not only produce such proof as the foregoing regulations direct in relation to widows' claims, but they must in all cases, as indispensibly requisite, show when they were legally married to the deceased officer or soldier on account of whose services the claim is presented, and that the marriage took place before the last term of service of the husband expired. They must also prove that they were never afterwards married.

7. In a case where the service of the deceased officer or soldier is clearly proved by record or documentary evidence, or the affidavit of a commissioned officer, showing the grade and length of service of deceased, the particulars in relation to the service are not required to be set forth in the claimants' declaration, except so far as to show that the claimant or claimants is or are the widow or children of the deceased.

8. The claimant must, in every case where there is no record or documentary proof of the revolutionary service of the deceased officer or soldier, produce the testimony of at least one credible witness. Traditionary evidence will be deemed useful in every such case.

9. Applicants unable to appear in court by reason of bodily infirmity, may make their declarations, before required, before a judge or justice of a court of record of the county in which they reside, and the judge or justice will certify that the applicant cannot, from bodily infirmity, attend the court.

10. Whenever any official act is required to be done by a judge or justice of a court of record, or by a justice of the peace, the certificate of the Secretary of State or of the Territory, or of the proper clerk of the court of the county, under his seal of office, will be annexed, stating that such a person is a judge or justice of a court of record, or a justice of the peace, and that the signature annexed is his genuine signature.

11. The widows of those who served in the navy, or as Indian spies, will produce proof, as nearly as may be, conformably to the preceding regulations, and authenticated in a similar manner, with such variations as the different nature of the service may require.

12. The form prescribed for claimants under the third section of the act will be observed by every other description of claimants, so far as the same may be applicable to their cases.

The judge or justice who may administer an oath, must, in every instance, certify to the credibility of the affiant.

13. In every case in which the deceased officer or soldier was a pensioner, the fact should be so stated, and the deceased pensioner so described as to enable the Department to refer immediately to the evidence upon which he was pensioned, and thus facilitate the investigation of the claim of his widow or children.

JAMES L. EDWARDS, *Commissioner of Pensions.*

ACT OF MARCH 3, 1837.

AN ACT explanatory of "An act granting half pay to widows and orphans, where their husbands and fathers have died of wounds received in the military service of the United States, and for other purposes."

Widow who has married again entitled to pension; provided she was a widow at the passage of the act.

Be it enacted by the Senate and House of Representatives of the United States in Congress assembled, That the benefits of the third section of the act entitled "An act granting half pay to widows and orphans, where their husbands and fathers have died of wounds received in the military service of the United States, and for other purposes," approved the fourth day of July, eighteen hundred and thirty-six, shall not be withheld from any widow in consequence of her having married after the decease of the husband, for whose services she may claim to be allowed a pension or annuity under said act; *Provided,* That she was a widow at the time it was passed.

Widows of those who continued in the service until Nov., 1783, entitled to benefits.

SEC. 2. *And be it further enacted,* That the widow of any person who continued in the service of the United States, until the third day of November, seventeen hundred and eighty-three, and was married before that day, and while her husband was in such service, shall be entitled to the benefits of the third section of the aforesaid act.

[Approved March 3, 1837.]

Pension Office, March 15, 1837.

In a case where the claimant has married after the decease of the husband, for whose services she may claim the pension, it cannot, under the explanatory act of March 3d, 1837, be withheld on account of her marriage, provided she was a widow on the fourth of July, 1836. The latter part of the 6th rule of the regulations of the 9th July, 1836, is not of course applicable to such a case. The facts in relation to the marriage of the last husband, on his death, should be fully set forth in the claimant's declaration.

The foregoing laws and regulations apply to the present war.

Rules 1, 2 and 3 are applicable to all claims of widows or orphans for pensions whose husbands or fathers may have died in the late war with Mexico.

ACT OF JUNE 19, 1840.

Be it enacted, etc., That in case any male pensioner shall die, leaving children, but no widow, the amount of pension due to such pensioner at the time of his death shall be paid to the executor or administrator on the estate of such pensioner, for the sole and exclusive benefit of the children, to be by him distributed among them in equal shares, and the same shall not be considered as a part of the assets of said estate nor liable to be applied to the payment of the debts of said estate in any case whatever.

ACT OF JULY 10, 1848.

The acts of Congress granting pensions to soldiers disabled by wounds or otherwise, while in the line of their duty in the public service, shall be construed to apply to the enlisted men of the Ordnance department, who have been or may be disabled, in the same manner as to non-commissioned officers, musicians and privates, of other corps of the army, subject to the limitation, that in no such case shall the pension exceed the rate of eight dollars per month.

2

By Act of 30th April, 1844, No pension shall be hereafter granted to a widow for the same time her husband received one; no person in the army, navy, or marine corps shall be allowed to draw both a pension, as an invalid, and the pay of his rank or station in the service, unless the alleged disability for which the pension was granted be such as to have occasioned his employment in a lower grade or in some civil brevet of the service.

But, by resolution, 23rd January, 1845, The above clause shall not be so construed as in any way to affect the claim of those widows whose application for a pension, or an arrear of pension, at the passage of this resolution shall have been made and filed in the Pension Office, awaiting the decision of the Commissioner of Pensions thereon.

By Act of 20th February, 1845, A pension shall not be granted to any widow for or during any part or portion of the time her husband may have received one, whose declaration therefor shall not have been made on or before the 30th of April, 1844, and shall not have been received at the Pension Office on or before the 25th day of January, 1845.

ACT OF MAY 7, 1846.

No widow, entitled to a pension under existing laws, and claiming a pension, whose husband was drawing a pension at the time of his decease, shall be required, in any such case, to furnish any further evidence that said husband was entitled to a pension; nor shall any evidence in any case be required, to entitle the widow to a pension, where the evidence is in the archives of the government, other than such proof as would be sufficient to establish the marriage between the applicant and the deceased pensioner in civil action in a court of justice; *Provided*, That upon a revision of the testimony in the case of the deceased husband, the Commissioner be satisfied that the pension was properly granted.

ACT OF JULY 21, 1848.

SECTION 1. The provisions of the first section of the act entitled "An Act granting half pay to widows or orphans, where their husbands or fathers have died of wounds received in the military service of the United States, in certain cases, and for other purposes," approved July fourth, eighteen hundred and thirty-six, shall be applicable to all widows and orphans of officers, non-commissioned officers, musicians and soldiers of the army of the United States, who were in the army of the United States on the first day of March, 1846, or at any subsequent period during the present war between the United States and Mexico.

SEC. 2. All widows and orphans of officers, non-commissioned officers, musicians, and privates, whether of the regular army, or of volunteers, who have died since the first day of April, one thousand eight hundred and forty-six, or who die, during the war with Mexico, from wounds received or from disease contracted while in the line of duty, shall be entitled to the same rate of pension as is provided for in the first section of the before mentioned act, under like restrictions; *Provided*, Said death has occurred, or may hereafter occur, while said officers, non-commissioned officers, musicians, or privates, were in the service of the United States, and in the line of duty; or while returning to their usual place of residence in the United States, after having received a discharge upon a surgeon's certificate for disability, while in the line of duty, or while on their march to join the army in Mexico; *And provided further*, That this act shall not be applicable to the widows and orphans of such officers, non-commissioned officers, musicians, or privates, who have not served in Mexico, or at posts or stations on the borders of Mexico; except where such officers, non-commissioned officers, musicians, or privates, have died while on their march to join the army of the United States in Mexico.

SEC. 3. All pensions under this act shall be granted under such rules, regulations, restrictions and limitations as the Secretary of War, with the approbation of the President of the United States, may prescribe.

ACT OF FEBRUARY 22, 1849.

The provisions of the second section of the act entitled "An Act amending the Act, entitled 'An Act granting half pay to widows or orphans, where their husbands or fathers have died of wounds received in the military service of the United States, in cases of deceased officers and soldiers of the militia and volunteers,'" approved July 21, 1848, shall be so construed as to embrace all widows and orphans of officers, non-commissioned officers, musicians, and privates, whether of the regular army or of volunteers, who have received an honorable discharge, or who remained to the date of their death in the military service of the United States, and who have died since their return to their usual places of residence, of wounds received, or from disease contracted while in line of duty, subject to such rules, regulations and restrictions as the Secretary of War, by the third section of said act is authorized to impose.

RESOLUTION OF MARCH 3, 1849.

In all applications for pensions by the widows of deceased soldiers, under the act of July twenty-one, eighteen hundred and forty-eight, the returns on the rolls of the disease of which the soldier died, and the official opinion of the Surgeon-General founded thereon, that from the nature of the disease contracted while the soldier was in the line of his duty, shall be considered satisfactory evidence thereof, without the proof now required at the Pension Office; and that it shall be the duty of the Commissioner of Pensions, in all cases of application for pensions under said act, to apply to the proper officers for said evidence, without requiring the applicant to furnish the same.

ACT OF AUGUST 11, 1848.

And be it further enacted, That all those widows, and such child or children, as are now receiving a pension under any of the laws of Congress, passed prior to the first day of August, eighteen hundred and forty-one, (excepting the law passed the third of March, eighteen hundred and thirty-seven), and those widows and children, who have received pensions at any time within five years prior to the passage of this act, may and shall continue to receive the same amount as they received under any special act, from the time such special act expired; *Provided,* Such act ceased on or after the first day of September, eighteen hundred and forty-five, or may hereafter terminate. And all such pensions as are now in force, and such as are renewed by this act, shall be paid out of any money in the Treasury not otherwise appropriated, so long as the said widows shall live as widows, and in case of the death, before or after the passage of this act, of the widows, to the orphan child or children of the deceased parties, until they respectively arrive at the age of sixteen years; and to the child or children of said widows in case of marriage by said widows, until said child or children shall respectively arrive at the age of sixteen years; and that the act approved 30th April, 1844, shall not be so construed as to exclude officers, seamen, or marines, from their pensions when disabled for sea service; *Provided,* That the whole amount received by the pensioner, including pay for his service and pension, shall not exceed his lowest duty pay. That the orphan child or children of the deceased parties shall have a pension in case the widow has died after drawing a five years' pension, to commence at the time when the widow dies, and to continue until the child or children shall respectively reach the age of sixteen years; and that any casualty by which an officer, seaman, or marine, has lost or may lose his life while in the line of his duty, shall be considered sufficient to entitle the widow's child or children to all the benefits of this act.

CHAPTER II.

OF BOUNTY LAND LAWS.

160 acre Land Warrant allowed to soldiers and those in the naval service, who have served in any war since 1790.

SECTION 1. *Be it enacted by the Senate and House of Representatives of the United States of America in Congress Assembled,* That each of the surviving commissioned and non-commissioned officers, musicians and privates, whether of regulars, volunteers, rangers or militia, who were regularly mustered into the service of the United States, and every officer, commissioned and non-commissioned, seaman, ordinary seaman, flotilla-man, marine, clerk and landsman in the navy, in any of the wars in which this country has been engaged since seventeen hundred and ninety, and each of the survivors of the militia or volunteers or State troops of any State or Territory called into military service, or regularly mustered therein, and whose services have been paid by the United States, shall be entitled to receive a certificate or warrant from the Department of the Interior for one hundred and sixty acres of land, and where any of those who have so been mustered into service and paid shall have received a certificate or warrant, he shall be entitled to a certificate or warrant for such quantity of land as will make, in the whole, with what he may have heretofore received, one hundred and sixty acres to each such person having served as aforesaid; *Provided,* The person so having been in service shall not receive said land warrant if it shall appear by the muster rolls of his regiment or corps that he deserted or was dishonorably discharged from service; *Provided further,* That the benefits of this section shall be held to extend to wagon masters and teamsters, who may have been employed under direction of competent authority in time of war in the transportation of military stores and supplies.

Those who have not received 160 acres entitled to the balance.

Proviso in case of dishonorable discharge.

Benefits extended to teamsters, etc.

Widow or minor children entitled to warrant.

SEC. 2. *And be it further enacted,* That in case of the death of any person who if living would be entitled to a certificate or warrant as aforesaid under this act, leaving a widow, or if no widow, a minor child or children, such widow, or if no widow, such minor child or children shall be entitled to receive a certificate or warrant for the same quantity of land that such deceased person would be entitled to receive under

Subsequent marriage.

the provisions of this act if now living; *Provided*, That a subsequent marriage shall not impair the right of any such widow to such warrant if she be a widow at the time of making her application; *And provided further*, That those shall be considered minors who are so at the time this act shall take effect.

Who are minors.

Actual engagement or 14 days service required.

And be it further enacted, That in no case shall any such certificate or warrant be issued for any service less than fourteen days, except where the person shall actually have been engaged in battle.

Warrants assignable. How.

SEC. 4. *And be it further enacted*, That said certificates or warrants may be assigned, transferred and located by the warrantees, their assignees or their heirs at law, according to the provisions of existing laws regulating the assignment, transfer and location of bounty land warrants.

How located.

SEC. 5. *And be it further enacted*, That no warrant issued under the provision of this act shall be located on any public lands, except such as shall at the time be subject to sale at either the minimum or lower graduated prices.

Compensation to Registers and Receivers.

SEC. 6. *And be it further enacted*, That the registers and receivers of the several land offices shall be severally authorized to charge and receive for their services in locating all warrants under the provisions of this act, the same compensation or per centage to which they are entitled by law, for sales of the public lands, for cash, at the rate of one dollar and twenty-five cents per acre; the said compensation to be paid by the assignees or holders of such warrants.

Provisions extended to Indians.

SEC. 7. *And be it further enacted*, That the provisions of this act and all bounty land laws heretofore passed by Congress shall be extended to Indians in the same manner, and to the same extent, as if said Indians had been white men.

Extend to those of the revolutionary war.

SEC. 8. *And be it further enacted*, That the officers and soldiers of the revolutionary war, or their widows or minor children, shall be entitled to the benefits of this act.

Battle of Plattsburg.

SEC. 9. *And be it further enacted*, That the benefits of this act shall be applied to and embrace those who served as volunteers at the invasion of Plattsburg, in September, 1814, also at the battle of King's Mountain, in the revolutionary war, and the battle of Nickojack against the confederated savages of the South.

SEC. 10. *And be it further enacted*, That the provisions of this act shall apply to the chaplains who served with the the army in the several wars of the country.

Chaplains entitled to its provisions.

SEC. 11. *And be it further enacted*, That the provisions of this act be applied to those who served as volunteers at the attack on Lewiston, in Delaware, by the British fleet, in the war of 1812–15.

Attack on Lewton.

[APPROVED March 3, 1855.]

On the 14th of May, 1856, Congress passed the following amended act, giving a liberal construction of the foregoing, and repealing the latter clause of section third. We have omitted the repealed clause. If a warrant for less than one hundred and sixty acres has been issued to a soldier, the fact that he served shall be considered settled and established, unless the Commissioner of Pensions, on examination, shall be satisfied that said small warrant ought not to have been issued.

SECTION 1. That in all cases where a certificate or warrant for bounty land for any less quantity than one hundred and sixty acres, shall have been issued to any officer or soldier, or to the widow or minor child or children of any officer or soldier under existing laws, the evidence upon which such certificate or warrant was issued, shall be received to establish the service of such officer or soldier in the application of himself, or his widow, or minor child or children, for certificate or warrant for so much land as must be required to make up the full sum of one hundred and sixty acres, on proof of the identity of such officer or soldier, or in case of his death, of the marriage and identity of his widow, or in case of her death, of the identity of his minor child or children; *Provided, nevertheless*, That if upon a review of such evidence, the Commissioner of Pensions shall not be satisfied that the former certificate or warrant was properly granted, he may require additional evidence as well of the term as of the fact of service.

Evidence upon which first certificate or warrant was granted, deemed sufficient to obtain the balance.

Commissioner of Pensions may require additional proof

SEC. 2. That in all cases where a pension has been granted to an officer or soldier, the evidence upon which such pension was granted shall be received to establish the service of such officer or soldier in his application for bounty land under

Proof of identity sufficient where a pension has been granted existing laws; and upon proof of his identity as such pensioner, a certificate or warrant may be issued to him for the quantity of land to which he shall be entitled; and in case of the death of such pensioned officer or soldier, his widow shall be entitled to a certificate or warrant for the same quantity of land to which her husband would have been entitled, if living, upon proof that she is such widow, and in case of the death of such officer or soldier, leaving minor child or children and no widow, or where the widow may have deceased before the issuing of any certificate or warrant, such minor child or children shall be entitled to a certificate or warrant for the same quantity of land as the father would have been entitled to receive if living, upon proof of the decease of the father or mother; *Provided, nevertheless,* That if upon a review of such evidence, the Commissioner of Pensions shall not be satisfied that the pension was properly granted, he may require additional evidence as well of the term as of the fact of service.

Widows and minor children.

Additional evidence.

Act repealed.

SEC. 3. That so much of the third section of the "Act in addition to certain acts, granting bounty land to certain officers and soldiers who have been engaged in the military service of the United States," approved March third, eighteen hundred and fifty-five, as requires the party claiming a certificate or warrant under the provisions of this act, to establish his or her right thereto by recorded evidence of the service for which such certificate or warrant has been or may be claimed, be, and the same is hereby repealed, and parol evidence, where no recorded evidence exists, may be admitted to prove the service performed, under such rules and regulations as the Commissioner of Pensions may prescribe.

Act of March 3, 1853 to embrace those in the naval service.

SEC. 4. That the eighth section of the act above mentioned, approved the third day of March, in the year eighteen hundred and fifty-five, shall be construed as embracing officers, marines, seamen and other persons engaged in the naval service of the United States during the revolutionary war, and the widows and minor children of such officers, marines, seamen, and other persons engaged as aforesaid.

Provisions to extend to those who have served 14 days.

SEC. 5. That the provisions of said act shall extend to all persons who have served as volunteers with the armed forces of the United States, subject to military orders, for the space of fourteen days, in any of the wars specified in the first section of the said act, whether such persons were or were not mustered into the service of the United States.

SEC. 6. That the widows and minor children of all such persons as are specified in the last preceding section of this act, and are now dead, shall be entitled to the same privileges as the widows and minor children of the beneficiaries named in the act to which this is an amendment. Widows and minor children.

SEC. 7. That when any company, battalion, or regiment, in an organized form, marched more than twenty miles to the place where they were mustered into the service of United States, or were discharged more than twenty miles from the place where such company, battalion, or regiment was organized, in all such cases, in computing the length of service of the officers and soldiers of any such company, battalion or regiment, there shall be allowed one day for every twenty miles from the place where the company, battalion, or regiment was organized to the place where the same was mustered into the service of the United States, and also one day for every twenty miles from the place where such company, battalion, or regiment was discharged, to the place where it was organized, and from whence it marched to enter the service; *Provided*, That such march was in obedience to the command or direction of the President of the United States, or some general officer of the United States, commanding an army or department, or the chief executive officer of the State or Territory by which such company, battalion, or regiment was called into service. One day allowed for every 20 miles travel to and from the place of enlistment. Proviso.

[APPROVED May 14, 1856.]

AN ACT to make Land Warrants assignable and for other purposes.

Be it enacted by the Senate and House of Representatives of the United States of America in Congress assembled, That all warrants for military bounty land which have been or may hereafter be issued under any law of the United States, and all valid locations of the same which have been or may hereafter be made, are hereby declared to be assign- Land Warrants made assignable.

able, by deed or instrument of writing made and executed after the taking effect of this act, according to such form and pursuant to such regulations as may be presented by the Commissioner of the General Land Office, so as to vest the assignee with all the rights of the original owner of the warrant or location; *Provided*, That any person entitled to preemption right to any land shall be entitled to use any such land warrant in payment of the same, at the rate of one dollar and twenty-five cents per acre, for the quantity of land therein specified; *Provided*, That the warrants which have been or may hereafter be issued, in pursuance of said laws or of this act, may be located according to the legal sub-divisions of the public lands, in one body, upon any land of the United States subject to private entry at the time of such location at the minimum price; *Provided further*, That when such warrant shall be located on lands which are subject to entry at a greater minimum than one dollar and twenty-five cents per acre, the locator of such warrants shall pay to the United States, in cash, the difference between the value of such warrants, at one dollar and twenty-five cents per acre, and the tract of land located on.

Proviso.

How warrants may be located.

Proviso.

Compensation of registers and receivers.

SEC. 2. *And be it further enacted*, That the registers and receivers of the land offices shall hereafter be severally authorized to charge and receive for their services in locating all military bounty land warrants issued since the eleventh day of February, eighteen hundred and forty-seven, the same compensation or per centage to which they are entitled by law for sales of the public lands for cash, at the rate of one dollar and twenty-five cents per acre; the said compensation to be hereafter paid by the assignees or holders of such warrants.

Entitled to same whether in or out of office at the passage of this act.

SEC. 3. *And be it further enacted*, That registers and receivers, whether in or out of office at the passage of this act, or their legal representatives in case of death, shall be entitled to receive from the Treasury of the United States, for services heretofore performed in locating military bounty land warrants, the same rate of compensation provided in the preceding section for services hereafter to be performed, after deducting the amount already received by such officers under the act entitled, "An act to require the holders of military land warrants to compensate the land officers of the United States for services in relation to the location of these warrants," approved May seventeen, eighteen hundred and forty-eight; *Provided*, That no register or receiver shall receive any compensation out of the treasury for past services who has charged and received illegal fees for the location of such warrants; *And provided further*, That no register or receiver shall receive for his services, during any year, a greater compensation than the maximum now allowed by law.

Fees.

Proviso.

SEC. 4. *And be it further enacted*, That in all cases where the militia, or volunteers, or State troops, of any State or Territory were called into military service, and whose services have been paid by the United States subsequent to the eighteenth of June, eighteen hundred and twelve, the officers and soldiers of such militia, volunteers, or troops, shall be entitled to all the benefits of the act entitled "An act granting bounty land to certain officers and soldiers who have been engaged in the military service of the United States," approved September twenty-eighth, eighteen hundred and fifty, and shall receive lands for their services according to the provisions of said act, upon proof of length of service as therein required; and that the last proviso of the ninth section of the act of the eleventh of February, eighteen hundred and forty-seven, (see 9th section, 1847,) be and the same is hereby repealed; *Provided*, That nothing herein contained shall authorize bounty land to those who have heretofore received or become entitled to the same.

Those whose services have been paid since June 18,1812, to be entitled to benefits of bounty land act.

Proviso.

SEC. 5. *And be it further enacted*, That where any company, battalion or regiment, in an organized form, marched more than twenty miles to the place where they were mustered into the service of the United States, or were discharged more than twenty miles from the place where such company, battalion, or regiment was organized; in all such cases, in computing the length of service of the officers and soldiers of any such company, battalion or regiment, with a view to determine any quantity of land any officer or soldier is entitled to under said act, approved twenty-eighth of September, eighteen hundred and fifty, there shall be allowed one day for every twenty miles from the place where the company, battalion or regiment was organized to the place where the

One day allowed for every twenty miles travel.

same was mustered into the service of the United States; and also one day for every twenty miles from the place where such company, battalion or regiment was discharged to the place where it was organized, and from whence it marched to enter the service. Computation of Time.

[APPROVED March 22, 1852.]

MILITARY BOUNTY LANDS.

Instructions to be observed by persons applying to the pension office for Bounty Land, under Act of March 3, 1855.

ABSTRACT AND CONSTRUCTION OF THE LAW.

PENSION OFFICE, March 5, 1855.

The act entitled "An act in addition to certain acts granting bounty land to certain officers and soldiers who have been engaged in the military service of the United States," approved March 3, 1855, entitles each of the surviving persons in the following classes to a certificate or warrant for such quantity of land as shall make, in the whole, with what he may have heretofore received, one hundred and sixty acres, provided he shall have served a period not less than fourteen days, and shall establish said service by record evidence, to-wit:

1. Commissioned and non-commissioned officers, musicians and privates, whether of the regulars, volunteers, rangers, or militia, who were regularly mustered into the service of the United States in any of the wars in which this country has been engaged since 1790.

2. Commissioned and non-commissioned officers, seamen, ordinary seamen, marines, clerks, and landsmen in the navy in any of the said wars.

3. Militia, volunteers, and State troops of any State or Territory called into military service, and regularly mustered therein, and whose services have peen paid by the United States.

4. Wagonmasters and teamsters who have been employed, under the direction of competent authority, in time of war, in the transportation of military stores and supplies.

5. Officers and soldiers of the revolutionary war.

6. Chaplains who served with the army in the several wars of this country.

7. Flotilla-men who served in the war of 1812.

Each of the surviving persons in the following classes are entitled to a like certificate for a like quantity of land, without regard to the length of service, provided he was regularly mustered into service, and shall establish the same by record evidence, to-wit:

1. Officers and soldiers who have been actually engaged in any battle in any of the wars in which this country has been engaged.

2. Those volunteers who served at the invasion of Plattsburg, in September, 1814.

3. The volunteers who served at the battle of King's Mountain in the revolutionary war.

4. The volunteers who served at the battle of Nickojack against the confederate savages of the south.

5. The volunteers who served at the attack on Lewistown, in Delaware, by the British fleet, in the war of 1812.

In addition to these classes, this act also extends to all Indians who have served the United States in any of their wars, the provisions of this and all the bounty-land laws heretofore passed, in the same manner, and to the same extent, as if said Indians had been white men.

Where the service has been rendered by a substitute, he is the person entitled to the benefit of this act, and not his employer.

In the event of the death of any person, who, if living, would be entitled to a certificate or warrant as aforesaid, leaving a widow, or if no widow, a minor child or children, such widow, or if no widow, such minor child or children, is entitled to a certificate or warrant for the same quantity of land such deceased persons would be entitled to receive under the provisions of said act, if now living.

A subsequent marriage will not impair the right of any such widow to such warrant, if she be a widow at the time of her application. Persons within the age of twenty-one years on the 3d day of March, 1855, are deemed minors within the intent and meaning of said act.

To obtain the benefits of this act, the claimant must make a declaration under oath, substantially according to the forms hereto annexed. The signature of the applicant must be attested, and his or her personal identity established by the affidavits of two witnesses, whose residences must be given, and whose credibility must be sustained by the certificate of the magistrate before whom the application is verified.

No certificate will be deemed sufficient in any case, unless the facts are certified to be within the personal knowledge of the magistrate or other officer who shall sign the certificate, or the names and places of residence of the witnesses by whom the facts are established be given, or their affidavits, properly authenticated, be appended to the certificate.

The official character and signature of the magistrate who may administer the oath must be certified by the clerk of the proper court of record of his county, under the seal of the court. Whenever the certificate of the officer who authenticates the signature of the magistrate is not written on the same sheet of paper which contains the signature to be authenticated, the certificate must be attached to said paper by a piece of tape or ribbon, the ends of which must pass under the official seal, so as to prevent any paper from becoming improperly attached to the certificate.

Application in behalf of minors should be made in their names by their guardian or next friend. Where there are several minors entitled to the same gratuity, one may make the declaration. The warrant will be issued to all jointly. In addition to proof of service, as in other cases, the minor must prove the death of his father, that no widow survives him, and that he and those he represents are the only minor children of the deceased.

If a party die before the issue of a warrant to which he would be entitled, if living, the right to said warrant dies with him. In such case the warrant becomes void, and should be canceled, and the next party entitled in right of the service claimed should make an application; and if there be no such party, the grant lapses under the limitation of the beneficiaries to the bounty. If the claimant die after the issue of the warrant, the title thereto vests in his heirs at law in the same manner as real estate in the place of the domicile of the deceased, and can only be assigned or located by said heirs.

Applications made by Indians must be authenticated according to the regulations to be prescribed by the Commissioner of Indian Affairs.

L. P. WALDO,

Commissioner of Pensions.

[The following act changes the previous practice of the Pension Office in regard to warrants issued after the death of the claimant:]

AN ACT declaring the title to Land Warrants in certain cases.

When proof has been filed during life of claimant, title of warrant to vest in the widow or heirs.

Be it further enacted by the Senate and House of Representatives of the United States of America in Congress assembled, That when proof has been or shall hereafter be filed in the Pension Office during the lifetime of a claimant, establishing to the satisfaction of that office, his or her right to a warrant for military services, and such warrant has not been or may not hereafter be issued until after the death of the claimant, and all such warrants as have been heretofore issued subsequent to the death of the claimant, the title to such warrants shall vest in the widow, if there be one, and if there be no widow, then to the heirs or legatees of the claimant; and all such warrants, and all other warrants issued pursuant to existing laws, shall be treated as personal chattels, and may be conveyed by assignment of such widow, heirs, or legatees, or by the legal representatives of the deceased claimant, for the use of such heirs or legatees only.

May be conveyed by assignment.

SEC. 2. *And be it further enacted*, That the provisions of the first section of the act approved, March twenty-two, eighteen hundred and fifty-two, to make land warrants assignable and for other purposes, shall be so extended as to embrace land warrants issued under act of the third of March, eighteen hundred and fifty-five.

Provisions extended in making warrants assignable.

[APPROVED June 3, 1858.]

CHAPTER III.

ACTS RELATING TO THE PRESENT WAR.

ACT OF JULY 22, 1861.

AN ACT to authorize the employment of volunteers to aid in enforcing the laws in protecting public property.

WHEREAS, certain of the forts, arsenals, custom-houses, navy yards, and other property of the United States, have been seized, and other violations of law have been committed and are threatened by organized bodies of men in several of the States, and a conspiracy has been entered into to overthrow the government of the United States, Therefore,

Preamble.

Be it enacted by the Senate and House of Representatives of the United States of America, in Congress Assembled, That the President be and is hereby authorized to accept the services of volunteers, either as cavalry, infantry, or artillery in such numbers, not exceeding five hundred thousand, as he may deem necessary, for the purpose of repelling invasion, suppressing insurrection, enforcing the laws, and preserving and protecting the public property: *Provided*, That the services of the volunteers shall be for such time as the President may direct, not exceeding three years, nor less than six months, and they shall be disbanded at the end of the war. And all provisions of law applicable to three years' volunteers,

Volunteers not exceeding 500,000 may be accepted to suppress insurrection, etc.

Term of service.

Disbandment.

shall apply to two years' volunteers, and to all volunteers who have been or may be accepted into the service of the United States for a period not less than six months, in the same manner as if such volunteers were specially named. Before receiving into service any number of volunteers exceeding those now called for and accepted, the President shall, from time to time, issue his proclamation, stating the number desired, either as cavalry, infantry, or artillery, and the States from which they are to be furnished, having reference, in any such requisition, to the number then in service from the several States, and to the exigencies of the service at the time, and equalizing, as far as practicable, the number furnished by the several States, according to Federal population.

To be called for by proclamation, and in proportion to population of States.

To be subject to army rules and regulations.

SEC. 2. *And be it further enacted*, That the said volunteers shall be subject to the rules and regulations governing the army of the United States, and that they shall be formed, by the President, into regiments of infantry, with the exception of such numbers for cavalry and artillery, as he may direct, not to exceed the proportion of one company of each of those arms to every regiment of infantry, and to be organized as in the regular service. Each regiment of infantry shall have one colonel, one lieutenant-colonel, one major, one adjutant, (a lieutenant), one quarter-master, (a lieutenant), one surgeon, and one assistant-surgeon, one sergeant major, one regimental quartermaster sergeant, one regimental commissary sergeant, one hospital steward, two principal musicians, and twenty-four musicians for a band; and shall be composed of ten companies, each company to consist of one captain, one first lieutenant, one second lieutenant, one first sergeant, four sergeants, eight corporals, two musicians, and one wagoner, and from sixty-four to eighty-two privates.

How to be formed

Infantry Regiments, how made up.

Divisions and Brigades;

SEC. 3. *And be it further enacted*, That those forces when accepted as herein authorized, shall be organized into divisions of three or more brigades each; and each division shall have a major-general, three aides-de-camp, and one assistant adjutant-general with the rank of major. Each brigade shall be composed of four or more regiments, and shall have one brigadier-general, two aides-de-camp, one assistant adjutant-general with the rank of captain, one surgeon, one assistant quartermaster, and one commissary of subsistence.

How composed and officered.

Major and Brigadier Generals to be appointed:

SEC. 4. *And be it further enacted*, That the President shall be authorized to appoint, by and with the advice and consent of the Senate, for the command of the forces provided for in this act, *a number of major-generals, not exceeding six, and a number of brigadier-generals, not exceeding eighteen*, and the other division and brigade officers required for the organization of these forces, except the aides-de-camp, who shall be selected by their respective generals from the officers of the army or volunteer corps; *Provided*, That the President may select the major-generals and brigadier-generals provided for in this act from the line or staff of the regular army, and the officers so selected shall be permitted to retain their rank therein. The Governors of the States furnishing volunteers under this act, shall commission the field, staff and company officers requisite for the said volunteers; but in cases where the State authorities refuse or omit to furnish volunteers at the call or on the proclamation of the President, and volunteers from such States offer their services under such call or proclamation, the President shall have power to accept such services, and to commission the proper field, staff, and company officers.

May be selected from Regular army, and retain their rank therein

Field, Staff, and company officers, how commissioned.

SEC. 5. *And be it further enacted*, That the officers, non-commissioned officers and privates, organized as above set forth, shall, in all respects, be placed on the footing, as to pay and allowances, of similar corps of the regular army; *Provided*, That the allowances of non-commissioned officers and privates for clothing, when not furnished in kind, shall be three dollars and fifty cents per month, and that each company officer, non-commissioned officer, private, musician, and artificer of cavalry, shall furnish his own horse and horse equipments, and shall receive forty cents per day for their use and risk, except that in case the horse shall become disabled, or shall die, the allowance shall cease until the disability be removed or another horse be supplied. Every volunteer non-commissioned officer, private, musician and artificer, who enters the service of the United States under this act, shall be paid at the rate of fifty cents in lieu of subsistence, and if a cavalry volunteer, twenty-five cents additional, in lieu of forage, for every twenty miles of travel from his place of enrollment to the place of muster,—the distance to be measured by the shortest usually traveled route; and when honorably discharged, an allowance at the same rate, from the place of his discharge to his place of enrollment, and in addition thereto, if he shall have served for a period of two

Pay to be that of same grade in regular army.

Commutation of subsistence and travel.

3

years, or during the war, if sooner ended, the sum of one hundred dollars; *Provided*, That such of the companies of cavalry herein provided, as may require it, may be furnished with horses and horse equipments in the same manner as in the United States Army.

Proviso.

Provision for volunteers wounded or disabled, or killed or dying in service.

SEC. 6. *And be it further enacted*, That any volunteer who may be received into the service of the United States under this act, and who may be wounded or otherwise disabled in the service, shall be entitled to the benefits which have been or may be conferred on persons disabled in the regular service; and the widow, if there be one, and if not, the legal heirs of such as die, or may be killed in service, in addition to all arrears of pay and allowances, shall receive the sum of one hundred dollars.

Pay of regimental bands.

SEC. 7. *And be it further enacted*, That the bands of the regiments of infantry, and of the regiments of cavalry, shall be paid as follows: one-fourth of each shall receive the pay and allowances of sergeants of engineer soldiers; one-fourth, those of corporals of engineer soldiers; and the remaining half, those of privates of engineer soldiers of the first class; and the leaders of the band shall receive the same pay and emoluments as second lieutenants of infantry.

Pay of wagoners, saddlers, etc.

SEC. 8. *And be it further enacted*, That the wagoners and saddlers shall receive the pay and allowances of corporals of cavalry. The regimental commissary sergeant shall receive the pay and allowances of regimental sergeant-major, and the regimental quartermaster-sergeant shall receive the pay and allowances of a sergeant of cavalry.

Chaplains, their appointment, qualifications and duties.

SEC. 9. *And be it further enacted*, That there shall be allowed to each regiment one chaplain, who shall be appointed by the regimental commander on the vote of the field officers and company commanders on duty with the regiment at the time the appointment shall be made. The chaplain so appointed must be a regular ordained minister of a christian denomination, and shall receive the pay and allowances of a captain of cavalry, and shall be required to report to the colonel commanding the regiment to which he is attached, at the end of each quarter, the moral and religious condition of the regiment, and such suggestions as may conduce to the social happiness and moral improvement of the troops.

SEC. 10. *And be it further enacted*, That the general commanding a separate department or a detached army is hereby authorized to appoint a military board or commission of not less than three nor more than five officers, whose duty it shall be to examine the capacity, qualifications, propriety of conduct, and efficiency of any commissioned officer of volunteers within his department or army, who may be reported to the board or commission, and upon such report, if adverse to such officer, and if approved by the President of the United States, the commission of such officer shall be vacated; *Provided always*, That no officer shall be eligible to sit on such board or commission whose rank or promotion would in any way be affected by its proceedings, and two members at least, if practicable, shall be of equal rank of the officer being examined. And when vacancies occur in any of the companies of volunteers, an election shall be called by the colonel of the regiment, to fill such vacancies, and the men of each company shall vote in their respective companies for all officers as high as captain, and vacancies above captain shall be filled by the votes of the commissioned officers of the regiment, and all officers so elected shall be commissioned by the respective Governors of the States, or by the President of the United States.

Military Board for examination of Commissioned officers of volunteers.

Effect of adverse report.

Proviso.

Vacancies in company officers, how filled.

Officers, how commissioned.

SEC. 11. *And be it further enacted*, That all letters written by soldiers in the service of the United States may be transmitted through the mails without pre-payment of postage, under such regulations as the Post-Office Department may prescribe, the postage thereon to be paid by the recipients.

Postage on soldier's letters need not be prepaid.

SEC. 12. *And be it further enacted*, That the Secretary of War be, and is hereby authorized and directed to introduce among the volunteer forces in the service of the United States, the system of allotment tickets now used in the navy, or some equivalent system, by which the family of the volunteer may draw such portions of his pay as he may request.

Allotment tickets may be introduced among the volunteers.

[APPROVED July 22, 1861.]

ACT OF JULY 25, 1861.

AN ACT in addition to the "Act to authorize the employment of volunteers to aid in enforcing the laws and protecting public property," approved July 25th, 1861.

Volunteers may be accepted in such numbers as the public exigencies demand.

Be it enacted by the Senate and House of Representatives of the United States of America in Congress assembled, That the President of the United States be, and he is hereby authorized to accept the services of volunteers, either as cavalry, infantry, or artillery, in such numbers as the exigencies of the public service may, in his opinion, demand, to be organized as authorized by the act of the twenty-second of July, eighteen hundred and sixty-one; *Provided,* That the number of troops hereby authorized shall not exceed five hundred thousand.

Provided, the number shall not exceed 500,000.

How to be mustered into service, armed, etc.

SEC. 2. *And be it further enacted,* That the volunteers authorized by this act shall be armed as the President may direct: they shall be subject to the rules and articles of war and shall be upon the footing, in all respects, with similar corps of the United States army and shall be mustered into the service for "during the war."

Appointment of Generals.

SEC. 3. *And be it further enacted,* That the President shall be authorized to appoint, by and with the advice and consent of the Senate, for the command of the volunteer forces, such number of major-generals and of brigadier-generals as may, in his judgment, be required for their organization.

[APPROVED July 25, 1861.]

ACT OF MARCH 25, 1862.

AN ACT to secure to the officers and men actually employed in the Western Department, or Department of the Missouri, their pay, bounty and pension.

Pay and bounty of soldiers of the Western Department.

Be it enacted by the Senate and House of Representatives of the United States of America in Congress Assembled, That the Secretary of War be, and he is hereby authorized and required to allow and pay to the officers, non-commissioned officers, musicians and privates, who have been heretofore actually employed in the military service of the United States, whether mustered into actual service or not, where their services were accepted and actually employed by the Generals who have been in command of the Department in the West, or the Department of the Missouri, the pay and bounty as in cases of regular enlistment.

Pensions to those of Western Department.

SEC. 2. *And be it further enacted*, That the officers and non-commissioned officers, musicians and privates so employed, who may have been wounded or incapacitated for service, shall be entitled to and receive the pension allowed for such disability; *Provided*, That the length and character of their enlistment and service be such as to entitle them under existing laws to such pension.

Proviso.

Heirs of such, allowed pensions.

SEC. 3. *And be it further enacted*, That the heirs of those killed in battle, or those who may have died from wounds received while so in service, shall be entitled to receive the bounty and pay to which they would have been entitled had they been regularly mustered into service; *Provided*, That the bounty and pay referred to in this act shall not be payable unless their term of enlistment and service be of such duration as to entlitle them to receive the same, according to existing laws.

Proviso.

[APPROVED March 25, 1862.]

ACT OF JUNE 23, 1860.

AN ACT to authorize the re-issue of Land Warrants, in certain cases, and for other purposes.

Land Warrants when lost new ones to be issued.

Be it enacted by the Senate and House of Representatives of the United States in Congress assembled, That whenever it shall appear that any certificate or warrant issued in pursuance of any law of the United States granting Bounty Land, has been lost or destroyed, whether the same had been sold or assigned by the warrantee or not, the Secretary of the Interior shall be, and is hereby authorized and required to cause a new certificate or warrant, of like tenor, to be issued in lieu thereof, which new certificate or warrant may be assigned, located, and patented in like manner as other certificates or warrants for Bounty Land are now authorized by law, to be assigned, located and patented; and in all cases where warrants have been or may be re-issued, the original warrant, in whose ever hands it may be, shall be deemed and held to be null and void, and the assignment thereof, if any there be, fraudulent; and no patent shall ever issue for any land located therewith, unless such presumption of fraud

Original to be void.

in the assignment be removed by due proof, that the same was executed by the warrantee in good faith and for a valuable consideration.

Rules to be prescribed for carrying this act into effect.

SEC. 2. *And be it further enacted,* That the Secretary of the Interior shall be, and is hereby authorized and required to prescribe such rules and regulations for carrying this act into effect as he may deem necessary and proper in order to protect the Government against imposition and fraud by persons claiming the benefits of this act, and all laws and parts of laws for the punishment of false swearing and frauds against the United States, are hereby made applicable to false swearing and fraud under this act.

[APPROVED June 23, 1860.]

DISCHARGING MINORS.

The practice of discharging minors who have enlisted without the consent of their parents would seem to be ended by recent legislation on that subject. An Act of Congress, approved February 13th, 1862, provides as follows:

SECTION 2. *And be it further enacted,* That the 5th section of the act of the 28th of September, 1850, providing for the discharge from the service of minors enlisted without the consent of their parents or guardians, be and the same is hereby repealed; *Provided,* That hereafter *no person under the age of eighteen shall be mustered into the United States Army,* and the *oath* of enlistment taken by the recruit *shall be considered final as to his age.*

The 5th section of the act of 1850 is as follows:

It shall be the duty of the Secretary of War to order the discharge of any soldier of the army of the United States, who at the time of his enlistment was under the age of twenty-one years, upon evidence being produced by him that such enlistment was without the consent of his parents or guardian.

AN ACT IN RELATION TO THE PAYMENT OF CLAIMS.

Be it enacted by the Senate and House of Representatives of the United States of America, in Congress assembled: That whenever a claim on the United States, aforesaid, shall hereafter have been- allowed by Resolution or Act of Congress, and thereby directed to be paid, the money shall not, nor shall any part thereof, be paid to any person or persons other than the claimant or claimants, his or their executor or executors, administrator or administrators, unless such person or persons shall produce to the proper disbursing officer a warrant of attorney, executed by such claimant or claimants, executor or executors, administrator or administrators, after the enactment of the resolution or act allowing the claim; and every such warrant of attorney shall refer to such resolution or act, and expressly recite the amount allowed thereby, and shall be attested by two competent witnesses, and be acknowledged by the person or persons executing it, before an officer having authority to take the acknowledgment of deeds, who shall certify such acknowledgment; and it shall appear by such certificate that such officer, at the time of making acknowledgment, read and fully explained such warrant of attorney to the person or persons acknowledging the same.

[APPROVED July 29, 1846.]

APPENDIX.

DECISIONS, INSTRUCTIONS AND FORMS

RELATING TO

PENSIONS, BOUNTY MONEY AND LAND,

ARREARS OF PAY, CLAIMS FOR PROPERTY LOST, ETC.

PENSIONS.

The following are extracts from the Opinions of Attorneys General, and from the decisions of the Secretaries of War and Interior respecting Army Invalid Pensions:

Descriptions of Disability which entitles the claimant to a Pension.

WASHINGTON, April 6, 1815.

The Secretary of War having, in a letter of the 4th instant, desired my opinion on the true meaning of the first clause of the fourteenth section of the act of Congress, passed on the 16th of March, 1802, for fixing the military peace establishment, I have the honor to submit the following:

The words of the clause are, "That if any officer, non-commissioned officer, musician, or private, in the corps composing the peace establishment, shall be disabled by wounds or otherwise, while in the line of his duty in public service, he shall be placed on the list of invalids of the United States, at such rate of pay, and under such regulations, as may be directed by the President of the United States for the time being."

The question made is, In what other way than by wounds must the disability have been incurred, to entitle the party to the pay provided?

The words of the section are not quite so distinct as to remove all grounds for diversity of opinion; yet, unless some liberality in their interpretation be allowed, it is to be feared that the benignant intentions of the law might be in danger of being curtailed or frustrated. The expression "or otherwise" is placed in contradistinction to wounds. In its primary signification, it may be taken to import a disability brought on by the direct and apparent agency of accidents or inflictions from the hand of God or man, happening to the party while in the immediate and obvious discharge of his duty, but which could not, with technical propriety, be denominated wounds. Instances of the kind may readily be conceived: as if an officer, while exercising his men on a hot day, should receive a stroke of the sun; a musician, while obeying an order to sound his bugle, should rupture a blood-vessel; or a soldier, while working upon fortifications should dislocate a limb: in such and similar cases that may be imagined, it cannot be doubted but that the disability would be brought on in a mode to meet the alternative stated in the act. It will be to enlarge it but a little more, and as it is conceived, to uphold its genuine and humane spirit as well as its legal sense, to say that the connexion between the inflicting agent and consequent disability need not always be so direct and instantaneous. It will be enough if it be derivative, and the disability plainly, though remotely, the incident and result of the military profession. Such are the changes and uncertainties of the military life; such oftentimes its toils as well as its hazards, that the seeds of disease, which finally prostrate the constitution, may have been hidden as they were sown, and thus be in danger of not being recognized as first causes of disability in a meritorious claim put forth for the bounty of the act. It would not, I think, be going too far to say that, in every case where an officer or private loses his health while in the service, to such a degree as to be disabled from performing his duty any more, he is contemplated *prima facie* as an object of this charitable relief from the legislature. I feel more doubtful in fixing, by any undeviating standard, what is meant by being in the line of his duty. Upon this point I should presume, however, that every officer in full commission, and not on furlough, must be considered in the line of his duty, although at the moment, no particular or active employment is devolved upon him. The same of a soldier who is kept in pay; for it is pre-supposed of both the one and the other that they are at all times prepared for duty; and it is surely of indispensible obligation upon them to keep themselves detached from other pursuits, so as to be ready, at a moment, to answer any call emanating from those who may be authorized to command them. Perhaps a voluntary absence, too long continued, on the part of an officer from his station, might form an exception, so as to exclude the idea of his having been in the line of his duty during any accident or sickness palpably proceeding from causes while he was away. But the officer who, by reason of marches in damp or cold weather, or who, from living in a garrison exposed to marshy exhalations, finds, even at some interval, his constitution broken down by rheumatism, or enfeebled by the constant recurrence of fevers, is surely as just an object of this humane stipend at the hands of the government, as he who may have had his arm shattered by a bullet. Such cases are again put only as examples. Others may also be supposed, in which the performance of military duty, in some of the various shapes it may be made to assume, has proved the original, though it may not be admitted as the proximate cause of the disability superinduced.

In the discretion which is vested in the President, a sufficient guard is established that an interpretation of the act, such as is indicated by the foregoing remarks, will not open the way to abuse. If the loss of health should have proceeded from careless or irregular habits in the party—much more, if from vicious ones; or if he brought to the service or ranks of his country a constitution already impaired, or rankling with the germ of maladies that afterwards do nothing more than ripen into activity; these will form occasions for caution, or for an entire exclusion from the bounty, when the executive duty comes to be performed in the way Congress have pointed out. A claimant who was suspected not to stand in lights altogether meritorious or innocent, must expect that his application would meet a severe scrutiny, and certain rejection at the discovery of anything that could taint it with unfairness or imposition. But if the sound construction be not at least as broad as I have supposed, we shall be at some loss to know what meaning the words "inferior disabilities," used in the concluding sentence of the fourteenth section, were intended to convey.

It may, perhaps, be said that, to earn the bounty, the disability should have been incurred by accidents or sickness peculiar to the employments of military men, and such as it may reasonably be supposed would have been avoided in other occupations. But it is conceived that this would prove a vague and deceptious rule of interpretation. With what safety or with what certainty could it be applied? The soldier asleep in garrison may suddenly, when he awakes, find his eyesight gone, without being sensible himself, or without its being imagined by others, that the predisposing and latent cause of his affliction was imbibed in ascending the Mississippi months before, while a hot and vertical sun was flashing its fires around him. Another may linger in a consumption, the consequence of perhaps a slight cold in the beginning, but of which the labors and hardships of his life may never have allowed him opportunity to get rid; and a third may lie bed-ridden under a palsy, which the change of habits and aliment after his enlistment may have been the chief, though occult causes in producing. It would be easy to multiply, indefinitely, such illustrations, applicable alike to the condition of officers and men.

I would remark, as giving strength to the principles which I suppose the legislature to have had in mind in framing this section, that we find it recorded in the Digest of Justinian, that "he who has hired his services is to receive his reward for the whole time, if it has not been his fault that the service has not been performed." So, too, by the maritime law it is well understood, that if sickness or disability overtakes a seaman, which was not brought on by vicious or unjustifiable conduct, he is entitled to his full wages for the voyage; nor does it make any difference whether it came on during the time he was on actual duty, or was merely accidental while he continued in the service. These principles have been sanctioned by time, and it is hoped that it will not have been deemed out of place to advert to the analogies they hold up.

RICHARD RUSH,

Attorney-General.

Endorsed.—The opinion of the Attorney-General is to govern in all cases of application for pensions.

A. J. DALLAS.

July 29, 1815.

WHAT CONSTITUTES TOTAL DISABILITY.

DEPARTMENT OF WAR, October 23, 1828.

SIR: In answer to your inquiry of this morning, I unhesitatingly give it as my opinion that the words "total disability," as used in the proviso of the the act entitled "An act regulating the payments to invalid pensioners," passed March 3, 1819, were intended as descriptive only of the *nature* or *character*, and not of the *extent*, of those disabilities; the biennial repetition of the proof of which is declared to be unnecessary.

The object of the enacting clause of this law, which contains but one section, is to oblige pensioners to exhibit proofs of the state of their respective disabilities at given periods, with a view to graduate the amount of the pension by the extent of the disability for the time being.

The object and spirit of the proviso is to save those pensioners, who are placed on the list in consequence of disabilities which are in their nature permanent and unchangeable, the trouble and expense of a useless repetition of proof; and they equally embrace cases (technically speaking) of partial and total disability. The word "total," therefore, as here used, in connexion with "disability," should not be taken in its technical sense, as indicating that extent of disability which entitles to a full pension; but in its ordinary sense, and conveying the same meaning as if the word *perfect*, or *complete*, or *permanent*, (for each of which it is often used as a substitute,) had been employed. The proviso, indeed, explains itself, by adding to the words "total disability" the following exemplification of its meaning, viz: "In consequence of the loss of a limb, or other causes which cannot, either in whole or in part, be removed."

If a soldier loses an arm or a leg, he presents a case of total disability, which entitles him to a full pension; and he need not repeat his proof, because the record shows that the disability is such as cannot, in the nature of things, be removed. But if a man lose only two fingers or two toes, it is a case of partial disability, and he receives only a part pension. It would, however, be equally idle and absurd to require him, in this case, to prove every two years, that his fingers or toes have not grown out again, as it would, in the other, to oblige him to show that his arm or leg has not been restored.

P. B. PORTER.

JAMES L. EDWARDS, Esq., *Pension Office.*

Invalid pensions, in all cases, shall be considered to commence at the time of completing the testimony, according to the provision of the second section of the act of 15th of May, 1820.

The evidence in support of pension claims is not deemed to be complete until decided on by the War Department. In future, therefore, the pension, in all cases, is to commence at the time when the decision is had on the claim, unless there has been a delay in the examination of the department; in which case, the pension is to commence at the time when the documents in support of the claim are received.

Affidavits or certificates in relation to invalid claims, whether original or for increase of pensions, may be received as evidence, if deposited in the department within three months from the date thereof.

Under the act of March 2, 1829, the widow or children of a deceased pensioner (as the case may be) must prove that they are such, before a court of record, and get a certificate of the fact from the clerk of the court, under his seal of office, before the arrears can be paid according to said act.

J. H. EATON.

APPROVED December 22, 1829.

Proof complete when the claim is decided.

JANUARY 14, 1830.

The Secretary of War does not consider the "testimony complete" until a decision is made on the case by the proper officer of the department. Where any delay occurs, imputable to the department, then no injury should result to the applicant. In this case, the delay was produced by no act of the government; of course, they can be allowed only to the time when the decision was made.

J. H. EATON.

A pension is suspended only for an omission to give proof of continuance of disability every two years.

ATTORNEY GENERAL'S OFFICE, December 9, 1831.

SIR: An invalid pensioner who had proved his title to a pension, and been placed on the pension list as such, has omitted for more than two years to produce the proof of two surgeons, as required by the act of March 3, 1819.

The question is, Can he be lawfully dropped from the pension roll on account of this omission? and must he offer again the proofs of his title to a pension, as if it were an original application, before it can be paid to him?

I think the act of March 3, 1819, does nothing more than suspend the payment until the proof of the surgeon is produced. In order, however, to entitle him to the pension for the whole of the time past, the proof must apply to his condition as an invalid at the expiration of every two years, and show that at those periods his disability continued. But upon offering such proof from two surgeons, in the manner prescribed by the act of Congress, he is entitled to the payment of his pension without again producing the evidence which was necessary, in the first instance, to entitle him to the pension.

But, a long omission to apply for payment and offer the proof, unless properly accounted for, may furnish grounds for suspicion, and would certainly justify a more rigorous examination into the claims of the applicant.

R. B. TANEY.

A person discharged as a minor not deprived of his right to a Pension.

FEBRUARY 10, 1836.

If a person enlists in the service, and while there, is disabled, and entitled under existing laws to a pension, and subsequently discharged before the expiration of his term, as a minor, I think he does not lose his claim to a pension.

LEWIS CASS.

Increase of pension on account of increased disability, to commence from the date of increased disability.

WAR DEPARTMENT, August 28th, 1845.

The practice of the department to commence the increase of an invalid pension on the day when proof is made of an increase of disability is very proper, and is in conformity with the principles laid down in the invalid pension laws; and the reason of the law is, that it is presumed in all cases that the claimant will perfect his proof as soon as his disability is so increased as to render it proper to ask for an augmentation of his stipend. But in a case where it is very obvious that the pensioner has suffered an amputation of a limb from a wound received in battle, and has, by reason of his helpless condition, arising from the loss of his limb, delayed his application, it is only just, and entirely consistent with the humane policy of the laws and a liberal construction of the same, that he should receive the pension, at the increased rate, from the time when the amputation took place. Let this be the rule, therefore, in the future, in every case where a pensioner has, after being pensioned, suffered the loss of a limb on account of a wound received while in the line of his duty as a soldier, receive the benefit of his increased pension from the time when the amputation was made.

W. L. MARCY.

A soldier is always in the line of duty, except under arrest, in confinement, on furlough, or absent without leave.

DEPARTMENT OF THE INTERIOR, April 10th, 1849.

Sir:—Your letter of the 30th ultimo, to the Secretary of War, in relation to the construction to be placed upon the joint resolution relative to evidence in applications for pensions of the 3d ultimo, has been referred to this department; and, in reply to your inquiry, have to state that it is my opinion, as a general rule, that the soldier is to be regarded as being always in "the line of his duty," when he is not under arrest, in confinement, on furlough, or absent without leave, although there may be peculiar circumstances in particular cases which should modify this construction.

T. EWING, *Secretary.*

DR. H. L. HEISKILL, *Acting Surgeon-General.*

Disability incurred from any cause by a person in the line of military duty, if not occasioned by his own misconduct, entitles him to a pension.

No person while in the receipt of pay or emolument as an officer of the army, can be placed on the pension list.

According to the order of the President, April 18th, 1829, the evidence in no invalid case, where the laws direct the President to prescribe regulations, shall be considered complete, until it shall have been duly authenticated; and no surgeon's affidavit or certificate shall be deemed evidence of disability sufficient to justify the issue of a pension certificate, unless the same shall have been received at this department within one month of the date thereof.

Where the death of a soldier is caused by intemperance, which is an offence against the military laws, he does not die from a disease contracted in the service and in the line of his duty; and therefore is not entitled to a pension.

Desertion forfeits all right to a pension.

Disability arising from cruel treatment by the enemy while a prisoner of war, entitles the disabled man to a pension.

An applicant for a pension is not entitled thereto unless he has been mustered into the United States service.

New proof will be required of invalids who have failed to apply, for two years, for their stipends.

A soldier discharged on account of a disease contracted, under which he was laboring at the time he entered the service, is not entitled to a pension.

Actual and not brevet rank regulates the amount of pension.

A widow's pension ceases from the day of her marriage, and the minor children, if any, are then entitled.

All invalid pensions commences from the time of completing the proof in the case. A widow's or minor child's pension commences from the day of the death of the husband or father.

A soldier who is injured by his own fault, is not entitled to a pension.

No one, while in receipt of pay or emoluments as an officer or soldier of the army, can be placed on the pension list. Pensions do not commence until the party is discharged.

A minor who has been disabled in the service, does not lose his right to a pension, although he may subsequently have been discharged because of his being a minor. A seaman was taken prisoner, and attempted to escape, for which he was severely punished by the enemy, and thereby disabled. It is held that the disability was contracted while in "the line of his duty," and for which he is entitled to a pension.

The pension of a minor child ceases on his arriving at the age of sixteen years.

OFFICIAL INSTRUCTIONS OF THE COMMISSIONER OF PENSIONS, TO BE OBSERVED IN APPLYING FOR AN INVALID PENSION.

All persons applying for pensions, by reason of disability incurred in the line of duty while in the military service of the United States, *must make a declaration, under oath, (or affirmation,) before some court of record*, setting forth the age and residence of the claimant; the service in which he was engaged; the time, place, and manner of incurring the disability alleged, with its precise character; and the date of his discharge; together with a statement of his residence and occupation since leaving the service.

In support of the averments of such declaration, the following rules must be observed in presenting the testimony:

I. The claimant's identity must be proved by two witnesses, certified by a judicial officer to be respectable and credible, who are present and witness the signature of the declaration, and who state, upon oath, (or affirmation,) their belief, either from personal acquaintance or for other reasons given, that he is the identical person he represents himself to be.

II. *The applicant must, if in his power, produce the certificate of the captain, or of some other commissioned officer, under whom he served, distinctly stating the time and place of the said applicant's having been wounded, or otherwise disabled, and the nature of the disability; and that the said disability arose while he was in the service of the United States, and in the line of his duty.*

III. If it be impracticable to obtain such certificate, by reason of death or removal of said officers, it must be so stated in the declaration of the applicant, and his averment of the fact proved by persons of known respectability, who must state particularly all the knowledge they may possess in relation to such death or removal. Then secondary evidence can be received. In such case the applicant must produce the testimony of at least two credible witnesses, (who were in a condition to know the facts about which they testify,) whose good character must be vouched for by a judicial officer, or by some one known to the Department. These witnesses must give a minute narrative of the facts in relation to the matter, and must show how they obtained a knowledge of the facts to which they testify.

IV. The surgeon's certificate of discharge should show the character and degree of the claimant's disability, but when that is wanting, and when the certificate of an army surgeon is not obtainable, the certificate of two respectable civil surgeons will be received, in accordance with the form on page 52. These surgeons must give, in their certificate, a particu lar description of the wound, injury, or disease, and specify how and in what manner his present condition and disability are connected therewith. The degree of disability must also be stated.

V. The habits of the applicant, and his occupation, since he left the service, must be shown by at least two credible witnesses.

VI. All evidence should be verified by oath, before a judge of the United States court, or some judge or justice of the peace, or other officer of a State, having authority to administer oaths for general purposes; and, if verified before an officer of any State, his official character must be duly authenticated; and such officer must, in all cases, certify that he is not interested in the prosecution of the claim.

VII. Attorneys for claimants must, in all cases, have proper authority from those in whose behalf they appear. Powers of attorney must be signed in the presence of two witnesses, and acknowledged before a duly qualified officer, whose official character must be properly shown.

JOSEPH H. BARRETT,
Commissioner.

Form of Application for an Invalid Pension.

STATE OF ——, } *ss.*
—— *County* }

On this —— day of —— 186 , before me, the undersigned, a [1]—— in and for the County and State above named, and by law duly authorized to administer oaths for general purposes, personally appeared [2]——, a resident of ——, in the State of ——, aged —— years, who being duly sworn according to law, declares that he is the indentical [2]—— who was a [3]—— in Company [4]—— commanded by Captain —— in the [5]—— Regiment of [6]—— Volunteers, commanded by Colonel ——; in the war of 1861 and 1862, for the suppression of the Rebellion, in certain States of the Union, and for the maintenance of the Federal Government. That he volunteered at —— in the State of —— on or about the —— day of —— 186 , for the term of —— and was honorably discharged at —— on the —— day of —— 186 , as will appear by his certificate of discharge herewith presented.

That while in said service, in the line of his duty, at ____, in the State of ____, on the ____ day of ____, 186 .[7]

That since leaving said service this applicant has resided at ____, and his occupation has been ____.*

He makes this declaration for the purpose of being placed on the Invalid Pension Roll of the United States, by reason of the disability above stated; and hereby constitutes and appoints ——, his attorney to prosecute this claim and procure a Pension Certificate.

(*Claimant's Signature.*)

Sworn to, subscribed, and acknowledged before me, the day and year first above named, and on the same day personally appeared —— and —— residents of —— and made oath that they are personally acquainted with [2]—— who has made and subscribed the foregoing declaration in their presence, and that they have every reason to believe from the appearance of the applicant, and their acquaintance with him, that he is the identical person he represents himself to be, that they reside as above stated, and are disinterested in this claim for a Pension; that since leaving the service of the United States, as aforesaid, his habits have been uniformly good, and his occupation ——.

(*Witnesses' Signatures.*)

Sworn to and subscribed before me; and I certify that I am not interested in this claim or concerned in its prosecution; that I believe the affiants to be creditable witnesses, and the claimant is the person he represents himself to be.

(*Judge's Signature.*)

STATE OF ——, }
—— *County.* } *ss.*

I —— Clerk of the County Court, in and for the County and State above named, do hereby certify that ——, before whom the foregoing affidavits were made, and who has thereunto signed his name, was at the time of so doing a —— in and for the County and State above named, duly commissioned and sworn, that all his official acts, as such, are entitled to full faith and credit, and that his signature thereto is genuine.

In testimony whereof, I have hereunto signed my name and affixed my official seal, this —— day of —— 186 .

—— *Clerk.*

All the "Discharge Papers" received by the soldier when discharged, should be sent with his declaration. The additional testimony that will be required to establish the claim, depends on the character of these papers.

The claim must be made before a *Judge of a Court of Record;* a Court having a Clerk and using an official seal being considered a Court of Record. The Judge can affix the seal of his Court to the affidavit, or the Clerk of his Court, or Secretary of State, must certify to his official character and signature. If most convenient, the claimant's declaration alone can be made before a Judge, and the affidavit of witnesses to his identity be made before a Justice of the Peace, or any other officer authorized to administer oaths for general purposes.

NOTES.—1. Here state the official character of the person administering the oath.
2. *Claimant's name;* his first name written in full.
3. *His rank* in the service.
4. The *letter* of his Company.
5. The *No.* of his Regiment.
6. The *State* to which the Regiment belonged. If the service was in the Regular Army the word "Volunteers" should be erased, and this blank filled with the word and letters: *Infantry U. S. A.*, or *Cavalry U. S. A.*, or as the service may have been.
7. Here give a particular and minute description of the wound or other injury, and state how, when, and where it occurred, or when, where, and how the disease was contracted, where the applicant has resided since leaving the service, and what has been his occupation.

In case the certificate of a commissioned officer cannot be had, insert the following after the *

And deponent further states that from the best of his knowledge, information and belief, the commissioned officers of the company in which he served, are either dead, removed so that their residences are unknown, or reside as follows, viz: Captain ——, at ——; Lieutenant ——, at ——; Lieutenant ——, at ——.

That in consequence of the foregoing, he is unable to obtain more full and correct evidence in support of his application than that herewith presented.

Captain's Certificate to Disability of Soldier.

(*Date.*)

I,[1] ——, do hereby certify that I am Captain of Company ——, of the —— Regiment of —— Volunteers, and am acquainted with [2] ——, who was a member of my Company, and as I am informed is an applicant for an Invalid Pension. That the said [2] —— was mustered into service on or about the ____ day of ____, 186__, and discharged for disability about the ____ day of ____, 186__, having become disabled from doing duty as a soldier from on or about the ____ day of ____, 186–, while in the service of the United States, and in the line of his duty as a soldier, in the manner and at the place, as follows:[3]____

That the said soldier was in good health at the time he entered the service, and the disability above referred to affected him while in the service and at his discharge, as follows:[4]____

NOTES.—1. Name of officer.
2. Claimant's name.
3. Here state distinctly the *time* and *place* of the applicants having been wounded, or otherwise disabled, and the *manner* in which it occurred.
4. Here state the *nature* of the disability.

This certificate may be given by *any* commissioned officer under whom the applicant served.

The surgeon's certificate for discharge should show the character and degree of the claimant's disability. When it fails to show this, or when it is wanting, the certificate of an army surgeon, or, in case the applicant does not live within thirty miles of a surgeon of the regular army, and this is not obtainable, the certificate of two respectable civil surgeons will be required.

Surgeon's Affidavit to disability of Invalid Claimant.

STATE OF—— }
County of—— } *ss.*

It is hereby certified that ——, late a ——, in Captain ——, Co. ——, of the —— Regiment of —— Volunteers, is rendered incapable of performing the duty of a soldier by reason of disease contracted while he was actually in the service aforesaid, and in the line of his duty as follows:

By satisfactory evidence and accurate examination, it appears that on or about the —— day of ——, 186—, being engaged at a place called ——, in the State of ——, he was disabled in the manner following, viz. [1] ——. That in consequence thereof he is now disabled, and the following is an accurate description of his disease and the manner in which it now affects him, and in what manner his present condition and disability are connected therewith, viz.: [2] ——. They further state that they believe his habits of life to be good, and not of a character to have produced or increased his present disease.

That he is in consequence of said disease not only incapacitated for military duty, but in the opinion of the undersigned is [3] ____ disabled from obtaining his subsistence from manual labor.

Dated the ____ day of ____, 186–.

(*Surgeon's Signature.*)

I certify, that the foregoing certificate was subscribed by ____ and ____ on the ____ day of ____, 186–, before me, the undersigned a [3] ____ and and for said County; and each being duly sworn, says that the contents of the same are true, and I further certify that the affiants are physicians well known to me, and that they are reputable in their profession. And I further certify that I am not interested in this claim or concerned in its prosecution.

Dated the ____ day of ____, 186__.

(*Signature.*)

1. The physicians will here give a full and minute description of the claimant's disease.
2. State here in what manner the applicant's present condition and disability are connected with the disease named, showing in what manner it has affected him so as to produce disability in the degree stated. If one of the witnesses was the claimant's attending physician before he entered the service, he should so state in this blank, and, if such was the case, that he was in no manner affected with his present disease before he entered the service.
3. This blank should be filled with the proportional *degree* of disability, whether, "*totally*," "*three-fourths*," "*one-half*," "*one-third*," or as the case may be.

Attach County Clerk's certificate to official character of officer who administers the oath.

PENSIONS FOR WIDOWS AND ORPHANS.

All widows of Revolutionary Officers and Soldiers whose husbands served six months in the Revolutionary War, are entitled to a pension.

All widows who have heretofore been granted a half pay pension for five years on account of their husbands' service in the war, are now entitled to a pension for life.

A widow of the second, third or fourth marriage is entitled to a pension.

By a recent decision of the Attorney-General, widows and orphans of volunteers called out under the act of July 22d, 1861, who die or are killed in service, are not entitled to the benefits of the act of 4th of July, 1836, and that no adequate provision seems to be made by existing laws for widows and orphans of volunteers.

Decisions of the United States Supreme Court.

A Pension was granted to the widow of an officer, conformably to the Acts of Congress, passed on the 6th day of July, 1836, and the 3d day of March, 1837, and she died before the Pension Certificate was issued; having disposed of her pension by will. Held, that the pension was payable to her executor, and not to her children, and that he was entitled to recover the same from the children, to whom it had been paid, by order of the Officers of the United States, who had charge of the matter of Pensions.

(*Foot* v. *Knowles ;* 4 *Met.* 386.)

Mrs. Decatur was held not to be entitled by the act of March 3d, 1837, to receive out of the Navy Pension Fund, half the monthly pay to which her husband would have been entitled under the acts in force on the 1st of January, 1835, in addition to the pension, for five years, granted to her by a Special Act of Congress, passed January 1st, 1835.

(*Decatur* v. *Paulding ;* 14 *Peters*, 497.)

Widow's Declaration—Half-pay Claim.

STATE OF ——, } *ss.*
—— County. }

On this —— day of —— 186 , before me, a —— in and for the County and State above named, personally appeared [1] —— a resident of ——, in the State of ——, aged —— years, who being duly sworn according to law, declares that she is the widow of[2] —— who was a[3] —— in Company[4] —— commanded by Captain —— of the —— Regiment of —— Volunteers, commanded by Colonel ——, and who —— at —— on or about the —— day of —— 186 , while in the service of the United States.

That she was married to the said[2] —— on the —— day of —— 186 , at —— by one —— a ——, that her name before her said marriage was ——, and that she has remained a widow since the death of her said husband. And she further states she believes there is —— public record of her said marriage, and there is —— private or family record.[5]

She makes this declaration for the purpose of obtaining the Half-pay Pension to which she is entitled by reason of the services and death of her said husband, and hereby constitutes and appoints —— her Attorney to prosecute the claim and procure a certificate.

(*Claimant's Signature.*)

Sworn to and subscribed before me, the day and year first above written, and on the same day personally came —— and —— residents of —— who being duly sworn according to law, declare that they are personally acquainted with Mrs.[1] —— widow of [2]—— who has made and subscribed the foregoing declaration, and were acquainted with her and her said husband before he entered the service, and know that they lived together as man and wife, and were so reputed. That she is the widow of the identical[2] —— who performed the military service mentioned in said declaration, and has remained a widow since his death. That their knowledge of the identity of her husband with the soldier is derived from[6] ——.

And they further testify that they reside as above stated, and are disinterested in this claim.

(*Witnesses' Signatures.*)

Sworn to and subscribed before me, and I certify that I am not interested in this claim, or concerned in its prosecution; that I believe the affiants to be credible persons, and the declarant is the person she represents herself to be.

(*Magistrate's Signature.*)

STATE OF ——, } *ss.*
County of ——. }

I, ——, Clerk of the County Court in and for the County and State above named, do hereby certify that —— Esq., before whom the foregoing affidavits were made, and who has thereunto signed his name, was at the time of so doing a —— in and for the County and State above named, duly commissioned and sworn, that all his official acts, as such, are entitled to full faith and credit, and that his signature thereto is genuine.

In testimony whereof, I have hereunto signed my name and affixed my official seal, this —— day of —— 186 .

——, *Clerk of the County Court,* —— *County.*

1. Claimant's name.
2. Soldier's name.
3. Soldier's rank.
4. Alphabetical title of Company.
5. *Proof of Marriage.*—If there is a County, Town or Church record of the marriage, a duly certified copy of such record must be sent. If there is no public, but a private or family record containing the marriage or the births of children, such private record should be sent. It will be returned when used. Parol evidence of the marriage is not admissible until the absence of record evidence is accounted for. If the testimony of persons who were present at the marriage can be produced, it should be sent; and if such testimony cannot be had, the declarant will so state. Testimony as to cohabitation and general repute as man and wife will not alone be sufficient proof of the marriage, unless the claimant is *unable to present either public or private record evidence, or the testimony of persons who were present, and so states in her declaration.*
6. Witnesses will here state in what manner they derive their knowledge of the soldier's identity, and if they or either of them were present at the marriage, it should be here stated.

PENSION OFFICE, *March* 15, 1859.

In a case where the claimant has married after the decease of her husband for whose services she may claim the pension, it cannot, under the explanatory act of March 3, 1837, be withheld on account of her last marriage, provided she was a widow on the 4th July, 1836. The latter part of the 6th rule of the regulations of the 9th July, 1836, is not, of course, applicable to such a case. The facts in relation to the marriage of the last husband, and his death, should be fully set forth in the claimant's declaration.

The following is the form of the declaration in such a case:

DECLARATION—*In order to obtain the benefits of the 3d section of the act of 4th July*, 1836, *and of the* 1*st section of the act of* 3*d March*, 1837.

STATE OF ——, }
County of ——, } *ss.*

On this —— day of ——, personally appeared before the —— of the ——, A. B., a resident of ——, in the county of —— and State (Territory, or District) of ——, aged —— years, who, being first duly sworn according to law, doth, on her oath, make the following declaration in order to obtain the benefit of the provision made by the Act of Congress, passed July 4, 1836, and the act explanatory of said act, passed March 3, 1837: That she was married to C. D., who was [here insert the particulars respecting the services of the deceased husband for whose services she may claim a pension, as directed in rule No. 4, of the foregoing regulations of July 9, 1836.]

She further declares that she was married to the said C. D., on the —— day of ——, in the year eighteen hundred and ——; that her husband, the aforesaid C. D., died on the —— day of ——; that she was afterwards married to H. B., who died on the —— day of ——; and that she was a widow on the 4th of July, 1836, and still remains a widow, as will more fully appear by reference to the proof hereto annexed.

She makes this declaration, [*etc., as in preceding form.*]

NAVY PENSIONS.

All officers, petty officers, seamen, and marines of the navy, who are disabled by reason of wounds received, or diseases contracted, in the service, are entitled to pensions. Also, the widows or orphan children of those who are killed or die of wounds received in the service and in the line of duty.

Form of Application for Navy Invalid Pension.

To the Commissioner of Pensions :

The memorial of the undersigned,[1] ——, who was a [2]—— in the United States naval service, respectfully showeth:—

That your memorialist was born at ____, in the State of ____; is ____ years of age, ____ feet ____ inches high; ____ complexion, ____ eyes, ____ hair.

That he entered the United States naval service at ____, on ____, and while attached to ____ and holding the rank of ____, he was disabled by [3]____. That the same was incurred by him in the performance of his duty; and having thereby been disqualified for the naval service, and disabled from obtaining his subsistence by manual labor, he refers to the evidence filed ____ and claims the benefit of the laws granting navy pensions ____, and that his pension may be made payable at the navy pension agency in ____.

(*Claimant's Signature.*)

Sworn and subscribed to, before me, this ____ day of ____ A. D., 18__.

(*Signature of Officer.*)

STATE OF ——,
County of ——, } *ss.*
Town of ——,

On this ____ day of ____, A. D. 18 , before me, the subscriber, a ____ in and for said county, duly authorized to administer oaths, personally came [4]____, aged ____ years, and [4]____, aged ____ years, whom I know to be residents of the County and State aforesaid, and persons whom I certify to be respectable and entitled to credit, and who, being duly sworn, say that they were present and saw ____ execute the foregoing affidavit by ____ to the foregoing declaration, and making oath thereto in due form of law, and they further swear that they are acquainted with the said ____, now present, and have every reason to believe from the appearance of the applicant, that he is the identical person he represents himself to be; and further, that they, deponents, do reside in the county aforesaid.

(*Signature of Witnesses.*)

WITNESS, ____

Sworn to and subscribed before me, this ____ day of ____, A. D. 18 , and I further certify that I am not interested as agent or attorney in the case.

(*Signature of Officer.*)

STATE OF ——, } ss.
County of ——, }

I hereby certify, that ______, Esq., before whom the foregoing declaration and power of attorney were made and acknowledged, and who has thereunto subscribed his name, was at the time of so doing a ———— in and for the county aforesaid, duly commissioned and sworn, and that his signature thereto is genuine.

In testimony whereof, I have hereunto set my hand and affixed the seal of ____ Court, for the county aforesaid, this ____ day of ____, 18__.

—— *Clerk of* ——

NOTES.—1. Claimant's name.
2. Rank.
3. Here give a minute description of the wound or other disability, stating distinctly the time, place and manner of occurrence.
4. Witnesses name.

Application for Increase of Navy Invalid Pensions.

STATE OF ——, } ss.
County of ——, }

On this ____ day of ____, 18__, before me, ____, a ____, personally appeared, ______, a resident of ______, who being duly sworn, declareth that he is the same person in whose favor a certificate of pension was issued on the ______ day of ______, 18__, under the signature and seal of the Secretary of the Interior, at the rate of ____ dollars, ____ cents per month, from the ____ day ____, 18 , and which pension has been paid him to the ____ day of ____, 18__, inclusive, at the Navy Pension Agency. That the disability for which the said pension was allowed was caused by ____ in the line of his duty, while attached to the United States ____, and holding the rank of ____, in the year 18__, and was graduated for ____ disability from manual labor; but that such disability having since increased, the said ____, for the purpose of obtaining a corresponding increase of his pension, requests that a Board of Survey may be ordered in his case, to be held at the United States Naval Station at ____.

Sworn and subscribed to before me, the day and year aforesaid.

The affidavit of two credible witnesses, as to the identity of the claimant, and the certificate of the clerk of a Court of Record as to the official character of the officer before whom the declaration is made, is necessary. See preceding form of application for a navy invalid pension.

Form of Application for Widow's Navy Pension.

To the Commissioner of Pensions:

The memorial of the undersigned [1] ____, the widow of [2] ____, who was a [3] ____ in the Naval service of the United States, respectfully showeth:

That the said [2] ___ entered the service in the year ____, and died therein, while holding the rank above mentioned, on the ____, by reason of [4] ____ in the line of duty.

That the undersigned was married to the said [2] ____ on the ____ day of ____, in the year ____, and that the following is a correct statement of the name__ and age __ of the child __ of such parties now living:____.

That your memorialist remain __ unmarried, and widow of the said____ to the ____, and referring to the evidence filed [5] ____ claims the benefit of the laws granting Navy Pensions to the widows of officers, seamen and marines, who have died in the Naval service, and requests that her name may be inscribed on the roll of pensioners, payable at the Navy Pension Agency, at ____.

SWORN AND SUBSCRIBED, before me on this ____ day of ____, in the year ____ }

(*Signature of Officer.*)

NOTES.—1. Claimant's name.
2. Husband's name.
3. His rank.
4. State cause and manner of his death.
5. State where the evidence is filed.

The affidavit of two credible witnesses, as to the identity of the claimant, and the certificate of the clerk of a Court of Record as to the official character of the officer before whom the declaration is made, is necessary. See form of application for a navy invalid pension.

Arrearages of pension may be paid to the orphans themselves, if adults, or to an administrator, for the sole and exclusive use and benefit of the children of the deceased parties.

Form of Application of a Widow in order to Renew her Pension under the Act of ——.

To the Commissioner of Pensions :

The memorial of the undersigned, the widow of the late ——, who was a —— in the Navy of the United States, respectfully shows :

That her husband, the aforesaid ——, entered the service of the United States in the year ——; that while in the said service, and holding the rank above mentioned, he departed this life, at [1] ——, on the —— day of ——, in the year ——; that the undersigned was married to the said —— on the —— day of ——, in the year ——, and in proof thereof, she refers to papers on file in the Pension Office, upon which she obtained a pension for five years. She therefore claims the benefits of the act of Congress of the ——, granting pensions to the widows of officers, seamen and marines, who have died in the service aforesaid; and she requests that her name may be inscribed on the roll of pensioners under that law, who are paid at ——, in the State of ——.

SWORN TO AND SUBSCRIBED before me, this —— day of ——, in the year ——.

The certificate of official character and signature of the magistrate who may administer the oath to be here subjoined.

1. If at a navy yard, the fact must be stated, and the name of the navy yard; if on board of a vessel of war, the name of the vessel must be given.

INSTRUCTIONS AND FORMS OF APPLICATION

For payment of Pensions upon Certificates issued by the Pension Office.

In case a pension has remained unclaimed by any pensioner for the term of *fourteen* months after the same has become due and payable, it cannot be paid by the Pension Agent, but application therefor must be made to the Treasury Department: if the certificate issued through the War or Interior Departments, (on account of military service,) to the *Third Auditor ;* if through the Navy Department, to the *Fourth Auditor* of the Treasury.

Digest of Official Instructions to Agents for paying Pensions.

1st. When application is made for the payment of a pension, the first thing that seems necessary is, that the identity of the person in whose behalf the pension is claimed should be established.

2d. Under the provisions of the acts of 6th April, 1838, and 23d August, 1842, where a pension has remained unclaimed by any pensioner for the term of *fourteen* months after the same became due and payable, it cannot be paid by the Pension Agent, but application therefor must be made to the Treasury of the United States through the Third Auditor, if the pension certificate issued from the War Department; and through the Fourth Auditor, if it issued from the Navy Department. Each Pension Agent, immediately on the expiration of fourteen months, subsequent to each semi-annual payment, will certify to the office of the Second Comptroller a correct list, containing the name, rank, rate of pension, amount due, and time of last payment of each pensioner remaining unpaid on the roll of his agency, whose pension has been due and payable for the term of fourteen months prior to the date of such certificate. When, however, a new pensioner is placed on the roll, or an old pension is renewed, the fourteen months commences running from the semi-annual payment next after the date of his, or her, pension certificate, and not from the commencement or renewal of the pension.

3d. When an attorney shall make application for a pension, *be the rank of the pensioner what it may*, he must deposit with you a power of attorney in his favor, duly acknowledged, and dated on, or subsequent to, the day on which the pension claimed became due, and within ninety days of the time of his applying for payment, and also his own affidavit that said power was not given to him by reason of any *sale*, *transfer*, or *mortgage* of said pension; and the execution of the power must be in the presence of at least one witness, other than the magistrate before whom it is acknowledged.

4th. In all cases of payments upon a power of attorney, the Justice of the Peace or Magistrate before whom the power is executed, must have lodged with the agent the certificate of the Clerk of some Court of Record, under seal of the Court, that he is legally authorized to act as such, and also a paper bearing his proper signature, certified to be such by the Clerk of some Court of Record.

5th. It is advisable, and is so recommended, that Pension Agents procure and place in a book the signature and seals of Clerks of the different Courts within their agency, who may be authorized to certify as to powers, the better to detect, by comparison of the signatures and seals, impositions that may be attempted.

6th. Under the provisions of the acts of 2d March, 1829, and 29th June, 1840, in case of the death of any pensioner, the arrears of pension due to him at the time of his death must be paid—

I. "To the widow of the deceased pensioner, or to her attorney," proving herself to be such before a Court of Record.

II. If there be no widow, then to the executor or administrator on the estate of such pensioner, for the sole and exclusive benefit of the children, to be by him distributed among them in equal shares; and the law of 1840 declares that the arrears of pension "shall not be considered a part of the assets of said estate, nor liable to be applied to the payments of the debts of said estate in any case whatever."

III. In case of the death of any pensioner who is a widow leaving children, the amount of pension due at the time of her death must be paid to the executor or administrator for the benefit of her children, as directed in the foregoing paragraph.

IV. In case of the death of any pensioner, whether male or female, leaving children, the amount of pension may be paid to any one or each of them, as they may prefer, without the intervention of an administrator. If one of the children is selected to receive the amount due, he, or she, must produce a power of attorney from the others for that purpose, duly authenticated.

V. If there be no widow, child, or children, then the amount due such pensioner at the time of his death must be paid to the legal representative of the decedent.

VI. When an executor or administrator shall apply for the pension due to a deceased person, he must deposit with you a certificate of the Clerk of the Court, Judge of Probate, Register of Wills, Ordinary or Surrogate, (as the case may be,) stating that he is duly authorized to act in that capacity on the estate of the deceased pensioner, and, if a male, that it has been proved to his satisfaction that there is no widow of the said pensioner living.

7th. In all cases of payments being made of moneys due a deceased pensioner, the original pension certificate must be surrendered, as evidence of the identity of the person to whom the pension claimed was due, or other substantial evidence of such identity must be produced in case such certificate cannot be obtained for surrendry, and that due search and inquiry have been made for said certificate, and that it cannot be found. The date of said pensioner's death must be proved before a Court of Record.

8th. A certificate of the facts proved must be obtained from the Clerk of the Court. It is not necessary for the Clerk to give the evidence in detail, but only to state the facts that have been proved, and certify under his seal of office that the testimony adduced was satisfactory to the court; and in case a pension certificate is illegally withheld from a pensioner, he (or she, as the case may be) must produce evidence of identity and the facts.

9th. When a pensioner is placed under guardianship, the Guardian applying for a pension must, in addition to the evidence of the pensioner's identity, deposit with you a certificate, from the proper authority, that he is, *at that time*, acting in that capacity, and also satisfactory evidence that his ward was living at the date the pension claimed became due. The identity of the pensioner, in such cases, must be established.

10th. For all payments made by you duplicate receipts must be taken, one of each you will forward, with your quarterly accounts, to the Third Auditor of the Treasury for pensions under the War Department, and to the Fourth Auditor for pensions under the Navy Department; and in *all* cases where a pensioner or attorney makes a mark from inability to write his name, there must be a witness thereto, otherwise such receipt or voucher will not be admitted at the Treasury.

Note.—By the second section of "An act making appropriations for the payment of the Revolutionary and other pensioners of the United States," approved February 22, 1840 Pension Agents are authorized to administer all oaths required to be administered to pensioners, attorneys of pensioners, or others, in the course of the preparation of papers for the payment of pensions under any of the laws of Congress; and to charge and receive the same compensation therefor as the laws of the State in which the agent is located allow to magistrates for similar services.

Decisions of the Second Comptroller of the Treasury, relative to the Payment of Pensions, by "Agents for Paying Pensions."

The references are to the volume and books in the Comptroller's Office containing the *decisions.*

1. The second Comptroller has no authority to decide on pension claims; that belongs exclusively to the Commissioner of Pensions.—*Vol.* 10, *p.* 353.

3. Pensions are payable to the persons named in the certificate, if living, and to the legal representatives of such as may have died.—*Vol.* 14, *p.* 21.

4. No deduction is to be made from the amount of pension due a deceased pensioner, on account of his indebtedness to the United States which accrued before the granting of the pension.—*Capt. Angus' case, May,* 1837.

5. If once placed on the pension roll, and thus acquired a legal claim to a semi-annual payment of a certain sum of money, the pensioner shall fail to assert this claim for six years, he cannot have his account audited without the authority of Congress.—*Vol.* 11, *p.* 107, 160.

6. When the War Department has given special directions as to the payment of a pension, it is the duty of the pension agents to follow the directions; and if payment be made, not in accordance with such directions, it cannot be admitted at the treasury to the credit of the agent.—*Vol.* 11, *p.* 403.

7. An invalid pensioner is legally entitled to his pension, although employed on hire in the service of the United States.—*Vol.* 14, *p.* 68.

8. The conviction and imprisonment of a pensioner for crime does not disqualify him from taking the usual oath of identity; nor does it deprive him of his right to draw his pension, or to appoint an agent to draw it for him.—*Dec. March* 20, 1852.

9. When an act of Congress directs the Secretary of War to make payment of a pension to the heirs of a deceased person, and that officer has issued the certificate in conformity to the law, the pension agent cannot pay over the money to any other person than the heirs, as expressly directed in the act.—*Vol.* 13, *p.* 30; *vol.* 12, *p.* 376.

10. The amount of pension due a pensioner under several acts of Congress, can be properly paid without a separate power of attorney under each act. One power of attorney will be sufficient, if it covers all the time for which the pension is due under all the acts.—*Vol.* 14, *p.* 141.

11. A pensioner may at any time revoke a power of attorney, which he has given for the collection of his pension, and demand payment to himself at the agency.—*Vol.* 14, *p.* 464.

12. By the 4th section of the act of July 4, 1836, the attorney of a pensioner is required to make oath, not only that he has no interest in the money by any pledge, etc., but also that "he does not know or believe that the same has been so disposed of to any other person whatever."—*Vol.* 8, *p.* 43.

13. The oath to be taken by the attorney of a pensioner claiming under the act of July 4, 1836, must be admisistered and certified by the agent who makes the payment or an accounting officer of the Treasury. *Vol.* 6, *p.* 195.

14. When a simple power of attorney is given to draw the money due a pensioner at a certain date, and the pensioner dies before the pension becomes due, the power of attorney is a nullity.—*Vol.* 9, *p.* 541.

15. The attorneys of commissioned officers who are pensioners, and of widows pensioned under the Navy Pension laws, are required to make oath that they have no interest in the money they are authorized to receive, "by any pledge, mortgage, sale or transfer."—*Vol.* 11, *p.* 356.

16. An attorney of a pensioner may take the required oath before a Notary, when the Notary is by law authorized to administer oaths in other cases.—*Vol.* 14, *p.* 2.

17. The term "legal representatives" of a deceased pensioner, as used in the act of March 2, 1829, means the executor of the last will and testament of the deceased pensioner, or the administrator on his estate.—*Vol.* 10, *p.* 428.

18. Arrears due a deceased pensioner may be paid to the administrator, unless some one or more of the heirs entitled, make known to the pension agent a preference that their shares should be paid without the intervention of an administrator.—*Vol.* 8, *p.* 359.

19. The Pension Act of 19th of June, 1840, was not designed to repeal the act of March 2, 1829, but it does authorize payment to an administrator, notwithstanding there are children living. Where there are no children living, the law does not apply.—*Vol.* 13, *p.* 28.

20. The Pension Act of June 19, 1840, provides that the pension shall not be considered as part of the assets of the deceased pensioner's estate, nor liable to be applied to the payment of the debts of said estate; therefore the amount of pension due at the time of the death of a female pensioner may be paid to her children, or to the administrator for the sole and exclusive benefit of her children, to be distributed among them in equal shares.—*Vol.* 12, *p.* 160.

21. When the executor or administrator of a deceased pensioner claims payment of the balance of pension due at the time of the death of a pensioner, the certificate of the proper court to the fact of the death will be sufficient, without certifying that there are children living. In the case of a male pensioner, it should appear by the certificate that there is no widow; as, in case of a widow surviving the deceased pensioner, she and not the executor or administrator, is entitled to the balance.—*Vol.* 14, *p.* 22.

22. On the death of a pensioner having neither wife nor child, the balance of pension due at the time of his death, is not payable to his half-sister, but to the executor or administrator on his estate.—*Vol.* 9, *p.* 637.

23. The balance of pension due a deceased pensioner at the time of his decease, is payable to the widow only, if she remain unmarried. The children have no legal claim to it, except in case of the death or intermarriage of the widow.— *Vol.* 9, *p.* 26.

24. A widow claiming arrears of pension due her deceased husband, must prove herself before a Court of Record, to be the widow of the deceased pensioner, and also take the oath that she is the identical person thus proved to be the widow.— *Vol.* 14, *p.* 19.

25. Where a widow, pensioned under the act of July 21, 1848, contracts another marriage, the agent must require her pension certificate to be surrendered, on paying her pension to the date of such intermarriage. If she has a child entitled to the reversion of the pension, application must be made with proper proof to the Commissioner of pensions, for a new certificate in the name of the child.— *Vol.* 13, *p.* 193.

26. By the acts of March 2, 1829, and June 19, 1840, the balance due a deceased Revolutionary pensioner, leaving children, but no widow, belongs to the children, and can be paid only to them, or to the executor or administrator, on the estate of the deceased pensioner for their benefit.— *Vol.* 11, *pp.* 16, 244, 190.

27. A widow pensioner, under the law of July 4, 1836, or July 21, 1848, is entitled to her pension up to the date of her death or intermarriage, if either occur within the five years for which the pension runs; and for the remainder of the time, if any, the pension inures to the child or children under sixteen years of age.— *Vol.* 12, *p.* 344.

28. On the death of a female pensioner, the balance of pension due at the time of her death is, by law, payable to her children then living.— *Vol.* 10, *p.* 5.

29. The share due each of the surviving children of a pensioner may be paid to his or her attorney, without the production of the original certificate, or a compliance with the regulation of Sept. 1, 1846.— *Vol.* 13, *p.* 25.

30. When a pensioner, who is a widow, dies, leaving children, the amount of pension due at the time of her death belongs not to the executor or administrator, but to her surviving children, to be distributed among them in equal shares.— *Vol.* 14, *p.* 38; *Vol.* 11, *p.* 104.

31. Payment of arrears due a deceased pensioner, who left no widow, must always be made to surviving children, if any, and not to representatives of children, who died during the lifetime of the pensioner.— *Vol.* 15, *p.* 426.

32. Children not being entitled to the pension, except upon the marriage of their mother; proof of her marriage and its date must be filed with their claim.— *Vol.* 13, *p.* 341.

33. When a child is by law entitled to the balance of pension due a deceased parent, the receipt of the child to the pension agent, is deemed sufficient, notwithstanding said child be a *femme covert* at the time of signing the receipt.— *Vol.* 11, *p.* 65.

34. Where one of the children named in a pension certificate dies unmarried, before the certificate is received, leaving brothers and sisters, the share of pension due him may be paid to the surviving children, without taking out letters of administration.— *Vol.* 12, *p.* 147.

35. Where one of two or more children named in a pension certificate cannot be found, and a certificate from the proper court, if offered as a voucher by the attorney of the other children, affirming that satisfactory evidence has been produced of the death of such child, or that he has been so long absent without having been heard from, as to be considered legally deceased by the laws of the State where he had lived, it will be considered sufficient proof of the right of the surviving children to draw the balance of the pension due.—*Vol.* 12, *pp.* 134, 146.

36. When several children are embraced in the pension certificate, the oath of identity is not required from all, but only from the one who may be authorized by regular power of attorney from the others to receive the pension money due.—*Vol.* 12, *p.* 87.

37. A grandchild of a deceased pensioner cannot, in any case, claim to receive the arrears of pension due the pensioner at the time of his death. If no widow or children survive the pensioner, payment must be made to the executor or administrator.—*Vol.* 14, *pp.* 44, 344.

38. At the death of the ward, the powers of the guardian cease. The balance of pension, therefore, due a pensioner who was under guardianship at the time of his decease, is not payable to the guardian.—*Vol.* 8, *p.* 65.

39. Whenever a navy pension has been unclaimed for two years, the application of the pensioner, and all the documents in support of his claims must be referred to the Fourth Auditor of the Treasury for investigation.—*Vol.* 8, *p.* 22.

40. Where an invalid pensioner's name has been continued on the rolls, and for a series of years he has not claimed the pension at the agency by producing the required proof of continued disability, and afterward produces that proof and claims under the original certificate, payment should be made at the Treasury. But if his name was stricken from the rolls of the agency so that he could not obtain his pension by applying there with the proper proof, and is to receive it by virtue of a new order from the Department, he should be paid at the agency.—*Vol.* 14, *p.* 63.

41. The pension agent may, if he thinks proper, require the attorney to receive the money at the office of the agency, though if it were paid on receipts executed elsewhere, the voucher would not be objectionable on that account.—*Vol.* 14, *p.* 221.

42. The regulations for paying pensions require that the certificate shall be set out in the application, and that the applicant shall make oath that he is the identical person named in that certificate.—*Vol.* 13, *p.* 123.

43. In cases where there is no county court seal, the pension agent will not reject vouchers for lack of the seal alone, but he will require the certificate of the clerk that there is no seal.—*Dec.*, *Sept.*, 1846.

44. A pensioner residing in Canada may execute his papers before a justice of the peace in the vicinity of his residence, if he is too feeble to cross over to the United States to have his papers authenticated.—*Vol.* 14, *p.* 125.

45. Where a pensioner neither signs nor makes his mark to vouchers requiring his signature, the pension agent is not authorized to pay the money.—*Vol.* 12, *p.* 509.

46. Pension agents may administer all the necessary oaths in the preparation of papers for the payment of pensions. By the act of February 19th, 1849, sec. 2, the deputies and clerks of pension agents have the same power as the agents to administer oaths.—*Vol.* 12, *p.* 219.

47. Notaries Public are not considered as authorized *ex-officio*, to administer oaths in the preparation of pension papers, but if the general authority to administer oaths has been conferred upon them by the statute laws of the particular State in which they reside and are commissioned, the oaths taken before them would be valid and of course respected by the pension agents. It should, however, be shown that such authority exists under the law of the State.—*Vol.* 12, *pp.* 1, 83. *September* 9, 1847.

48. It is required by the proviso in the first section of the act of September 16th, 1850, chap. 52, that the official character of a notary shall be established by other evidence than his seal and signature. The proviso in the first section applies only to cases where the notary has certified that oaths or affirmations were taken before him, and not to certificates of acknowledgment of instruments.—*Vol.* 14, *p.* 111.

49. A pension agent must require that the certificates should be set out in the oath of identity.—*Vol.* 13, *p.* 21.

50. The omission of the words "duly authorized by law to administer oaths" from the oath of identity or acknowledgment of the power of attorney in the pension papers, is not so important as to render it necessary to reject the papers on that account.—*Vol.* 11, *pp.* 404, 423, 437.

51. By the act of the General Assembly of the State of Ohio, passed March 22, 1849, notaries are authorized to administer oaths in all cases where an oath is required in the execution of papers to draw pensions at the pension agencies or at the Treasury of the United States.—*Vol.* 14, *p.* 62.

52. That section of the pension instructions which requires a witness to pension vouchers where the pensioner or attorney of a pensioner subscribes by a mark in consequence of inability to write, applies to the oath of identity as well as to every other necessary voucher. In all cases, therefore, a witness is required, other than, and in addition to the magistrate before whom the affidavit is made.—*Vol.* 12, *p.* 85.

53. A power of attorney to draw a pension must be dated and acknowledged on, or subsequent to the day on which the pension becomes due. —*Vol.* 14, *pp.* 228, 430: *Vol.* 13, *pp.* 123, 287, 291.

54. When interlineations and additions are made in a power of attorney to draw a pension, they must be noted by the magistrate.—*Vol.* 6, *p.* 44.

55. When a pensioner receives from the pension agent a greater sum than was his due, the excess should stand to his debit, and be considered as so much paid, and no further payment should be made until something shall become due, after deducting the sum so over paid. —*Vol.* 8, *pp.* 222, 421.

56. A power of attorney to draw a pension is not vitiated in consequence of its giving authority to draw for a time antecedent to that from which the pension is due.—*Vol.* 14, *p.* 88.

57. If the pension agent pay to the attorney more money than the pensioner authorized the attorney to receive, the pensioner is not legally accountable for the excess unless it be shown that he received such excess, or sanctioned the act of the attorney in so receiving it.—*Vol.* 8, *p.* 438.

58. On the application of a guardian for the payment of a pension due his wards, he must furnish proof that they are still living, are under twenty-one years of age, and that he still continues to be their guardian. —*Vol.* 8, *p.* 25.

Application of Invalid Pensioner for Payment of Pension.

STATE OF ——, } *ss.*
County of ——, }

BE IT KNOWN, That before me ——, a Justice of the Peace, in and for the County and State aforesaid, duly authorized by law to administer oaths for general purposes, personally appeared —— and made oath in due form of law that he is the identical person named in an original certificate in his possession, of which I certify the following is a true copy:

(*Here insert a copy of his Certificate of Pension.*)

That the said —— now resides in ——, and has resided there for the space of — years past; and that previous thereto he resided in ——, and that he has not been employed, or paid in the army, navy or marine service of the United States from —— till ——, of the truth of which statement I am fully satisfied.

Witness :—— (*Signature of Claimant.*)
Witness :——

Sworn to and subscribed before me this —— day of ——, A D. 186 .

—— *J. P.*

KNOW ALL MEN BY THESE PRESENTS, That —— of ——, in the State of —— do hereby constitute and appoint —— my true and lawful Attorney, for me, and in my name, to receive from the Agent of the United States for paying pensions in —— State of —— my pension from the — day of —— 18— to the — day of ——, 18—.

Witness my hand and seal this —— day of ——, 18—.
Sealed and delivered in presence of

Witness :—— ——(*Seal.*)
Witness :——

STATE OF ——, } *ss.*
County of ——, }

BE IT KNOWN, That on this —— day of ——, 18—, before me, —— a Justice of the Peace, in and for the County and State aforesaid, personally appeared ____ above named, and acknowledged the foregoing power of Attorney to be his act and deed. In testimony whereof, I have hereunto set my hand the day and year last above written.

—— *J. P.*

STATE OF ____, } ss.
County of ____, }

BE IT KNOWN, That on the ____ day of ____, 18__, before me a ____, duly authorized by law to administer oaths for general purposes, personally appeared ____, the Attorney named in the foregoing power of attorney, and made oath that he has no interest whatever in the money he is authorized to receive by virtue of the foregoing power of attorney, either by any pledge, mortgage, sale, assignment or transfer, and that he does not know or believe that the same has been so disposed of to any person whatever.

(*Signature of Attorney.*)

Sworn and subscribed, the day and year last above mentioned before me,

______ *J. P.*

STATE OF ____, } ss.
County of ____, }

I ____, Clerk of the ____ County Court, do hereby certify that ____, Esq., before whom the foregoing declaration and power of attorney were made, and who has thereunto subscribed his name, was at the time of so doing a Justice of the Peace, in and for the State and County aforesaid, duly commissioned and sworn, and that his signature thereto is genuine.

In testimony whereof, I have hereunto signed my name and affixed my official seal, this ____ day ____, 18__.

——, *Clerk.*

Widow's Application.

STATE OF ____, } ss.
County of ____, }

BE IT KNOWN, That before me, ____, a Justice of the Peace, in and for the county aforesaid, duly authorized by law to administer oaths, personally appeared ____, widow of ____, and made oath in due form of law, that she is the identical person named in an original certificate in her possession, of which (I certify) the following is a true copy:

(*Here insert a copy of her Certificate of Pension.*)

That she has not intermarried, but continues the widow of the above mentioned ____, and that she now resides in ____, and has resided there for the space of __ years past; and that previous thereto she resided in ____; of the truth of which statement I am fully satisfied.

Witness : ——— (*Claimant's Signature.*)
Witness : ———

Sworn and subscribed before me this ____day of ____ , A. D. 18__.

—— *J. P.*

KNOW ALL MEN BY THESE PRESENTS, That ____, of ____, a revolutionary pensioner, do hereby constitute and appoint ____, true and lawful attorney, for ____, and in ____ name, to receive from the agent of the United States for paying pensions in ____, State of ____, my pension from the ____ day of ____, 18__, to the ____ day of ____ 18__.

Witness ____ hand and seal, this ____ day of ____, 18__.

Sealed and delivered in presence of

Witness: ———— ———— (*Seal.*)
Witness: ————

STATE OF ____, }
County of ____, } *ss.*

BE IT KNOWN, That on the ____ day of ____, 18__, before the subscriber, a Justice of the Peace in and for said county, personally appeared ____, aboved named, and acknowledged the foregoing power of attorney to be ____ act and deed. In testimony whereof, I have hereunto set my hand the day and year last above mentioned.

———— *J. P.*

STATE OF ____, }
County of ____, } *ss.*

BE IT KNOWN, That on the ____ day of ____, 18__, before me, a ____, duly authorized, by the laws of the State to administer oaths, personally appeared ____, the attorney named in the foregoing power of attorney, and made oath that he has no interest whatever in the money he is authorized to receive by virtue of the foregoing power of attorney, either by any pledge, mortgage, sale, assignment, or transfer, and that he does not know or believe that the same has been so disposed of to any person whatever.

(*Signature of Attorney.*)

Sworn and subscribed, the day and year last above mentioned, before me.

———— *J. P.*

STATE OF ____, }
County of ____, } *to wit:*

I HEREBY CERTIFY, That ____, Esq., before whom the foregoing declaration and power of attorney were made, and who has thereunto subscribed his name, was at the time of so doing a Justice of the Peace, in and for the county aforesaid, duly commissioned and sworn, and that his signature thereto is genuine.

IN TESTIMONY WHEREOF, I have hereunto signed my name and affixed the seal of ____, for the County aforesaid, this ____ day of ____, 18__.

————, *Clerk.*

Guardian's Application.

STATE OF ——, }
County of——, } *ss.*

BE IT KNOWN, That before me ——, a Justice of the Peace, in and for the county aforesaid, duly authorized by law to administer oaths, personally appeared —— guardian of [1] ——, and made oath in due form of law, that the said [1] —— is still living, and is the identical person named in an original certificate in his possession, of which (I certify) the following is a true copy:

(*Here insert a copy of the certificate.*)

That —— now resides in —— and has resided there for the space of —— years past; and that previous thereto —— resided in ——; of the truth of which statement I am fully satisfied.

Witness:——
Witness:—— ——(*Guardian.*)

Sworn to and subscribed before me, this —— day of ——, A. D. 18 .

——, *J. P.*

KNOW ALL MEN BY THESE PRESENTS, That ——, of ——, guardian of [1]——, do hereby constitute and appoint —— my true and lawful attorney, for ——, and in —— name, to receive from the agent of the pension of —— from the —— day of ——, 18—, to the —— day of —— the United States for paying pensions in ——, State of ——, 18—.

Witness —— hand and seal, this —— day of——, 18—.

Sealed and delivered in presence of

Witness:——
Witness:—— ——(*Seal.*)

STATE OF ——, }
County of ——, } *ss.*

BE IT KNOWN, That on the —— day of ——, 18—, before the subscriber, a Justice of the Peace, in and for said county, personally appeared —— above named, and acknowledged the foregoing power of attorney to be ——, act and deed. In testimony whereof, I have hereunto set my hand the day and year last above mentioned.

——, *J. P.*

STATE OF ——, }
County of ——, } *ss.*

BE IT KNOWN, That on the —— day of——, 18—, before me, a ——, duly authorized by the laws of the State to administer oaths, personally appeared ——, the attorney named in the foregoing power of attorney, and made oath that he has no interest whatever in the money he is authorized to receive by virtue of the foregoing power of attorney, either by any pledge, mortgage, sale, assignment or transfer, and that he does not know or believe that the same has been so disposed of by any person whatever.

Sworn and subscribed the day and year last above mentioned, before me.

——*J. P.*

STATE OF ____, }
County of ____, } *to wit:*

I HEREBY CERTIFY that ____, Esq., before whom the foregoing declaration and power of attorney were made, and who has thereunto subscribed his name, was, at the time of so doing, a Justice of the Peace, in and for the county aforesaid, duly commissioned and sworn, and that his signature thereto is genuine, and that ____ is guardian of ____, duly qualified to act as such.

In testimony whereof, I have hereunto signed my name and affixed the seal of the ____, for the county aforesaid, this ____ day of ____, 18__.

______, *Clerk.*

NOTE. 1.—Pensioner's name.

DECEASED PENSIONERS.

Form of Application for the Widow or Child of a Deceased Pensioner.

[In case the pension has been due and unclaimed for *fourteen* months, the application should be presented to the third auditor of the Treasury; if less than fourteen months, at the agency where the certificate is made payable.]

STATE OF ____, }
County of ____, } *ss.*

BE IT KNOWN, That before me, ____, a ____, in and for the county aforesaid, duly authorized by law to administer oaths, personally appeared ____, and made oath in due form of law, that she (or he, as the case may be) is the widow (or son, or daughter, as the case may be,) of ____ the identical person who was a pensioner, and is now dead, and to whom a certificate of pension was issued, which is herewith surrendered. [1]

That the deceased pensioner resided in ____, in the State of ____, for the space of ____ years before his death; and that previous thereto he resided in ____.

Sworn and subscribed this ____ day of ____, 18__, before me.

______

NOTE.—The above deposition must be signed by the deponent. Where the pension has been increased, since the certificate has been given, the magistrate will note the fact.

The oath of identity for the Executor or Administrator of a deceased pensioner may be in the foregoing form—substituting "Executor" (or "Administrator," as the case may be) for "widow," etc.

Power of Attorney for the Widow or Child of a Deceased Pensioner.

KNOW ALL MEN BY THESE PRESENTS, That I, ____, of ____, in the county of ____, State of ____, widow (or child, as the case may be,) of ______, who was an invalid pensioner of the United States, do hereby constitute and appoint ____, my true and lawful attorney, for me, and in my name, to receive from the agent of the United States for paying pensions in ___ State of ____, the balance of said pension from the ____ day of ____, 18__, to the ____ day of ____, being the day of his death.

Witness my hand and seal, this ____ day of, ____, 18__.

Sealed and delivered in presence of

Witness :——— ———[SEAL.]

Witness :———

NOTES. When one of the children is appointed by the others to receive the balance, the Attorney's oath is not required.

1. In case the pension certificate has been lost, insert, immediately after the name, or names, of the widow, child or children, as the case may be, the following: "And that the pension certificate of said pensioner has been lost, and, after due search and inquiry therefor, it cannot be found."

———

Certificate of the Court as to the Death of a Pensioner.

STATE OF ———, }
County of ———, } *ss.*

I, ____, Clerk of the Court of ____, holden at ____, in and for ____, do hereby certify, that satisfactory evidence has been exhibited to said Court that ____ was a pensioner of the United States at the rate of ____ dollars per ____; was a resident of the County of ____, in the State of ____ and died in the ____, in the State of ____, in the year ____, on the ____ day of ____; that he left a widow [or no widow] (or child or children, as the case may be) whose name is (or are, as the case may be,)——

In testimony whereof, I have hereunto set my hand and affixed my seal [Seal of the Court.] ____ of office at ____, this ____ day of ____, in the year of our Lord 18—.

———, *Clerk of the* ———

———

Application for a New Certificate.

STATE OF ———, }
County of ———, } *ss.*

On this ____ day of ____, A. D. 186 , before me, the subscriber, a Justice of the Peace in and for the said county of ____ personally appeared ____, who, on his oath, declares that he is the same person who formerly belonged to the company commanded by Captain ____, in the regiment commanded by Colonel ____, in the service of the United States; that his name was placed on the pension roll of the State of ____ that he received a *certificate of that fact under the signature and seal of the Secretary of War*,[1] (or Secretary of the Interior;) which certificate on or about the ____ day of ____, 186 , at or near ____.

(*Here state the time, place, and manner of the loss or destruction of the certificate.*)

(*Claimant's Signature.*)

Sworn to and subscribed before me, this ___ day of ___, A. D. 186

——*J. P.*

STATE OF ______,
County of ______, ss.
Town of ______,

On this ___ day of ___, A. D. 186–, before me, the subscriber, a ___ in and for said County, duly authorized to administer oaths, personally came ___, aged ___ years, and ___, aged ___ years, whom I know to to be residents of the County and State aforesaid, and persons whom I certify to be respectable and entitled to credit, and who, being duly sworn, say that they were present and saw ___ execute the foregoing affidavit by ___ to the foregoing declaration, and making oath thereto in due form of law, and they further swear that they are acquainted with said ___ now present, and that he is the identical person he represents himself to be; and further, that they, deponents, do reside in the County aforesaid.

(*Witnesses' Signatures.*)

Sworn to and subscribed before me, this ___ day of ___ A. D. 186–, and I certify that I have no interest in this case as attorney, or otherwise.

——*J. P.*

STATE OF ______,
County of ______, ss.

I hereby certify, that ___, Esq., before whom the foregoing Declaration and Power of Attorney were made and acknowledged, and who has thereunto subscribed his name, was at the time of so doing a Justice of the Peace, in and for the County aforesaid, duly commissioned and sworn, and that his signature thereto is genuine.

In testimony whereof, I have hereunto set my hand and affixed the seal of ___ Court, for the County aforesaid, this ___ day of ___, 186–.

—— *Clerk.*

1. If the pensioner has never received a formal certificate, but has drawn his pension on a mere notification, as was the case in a few instances many years ago, he should leave out the above words in *Italics*, and insert in lieu thereof, "*but has never received a formal certificate, and now wishes to obtain one.*"

The oath to be taken before a duly qualified magistrate, whose official character and signature must be properly authenticated.

The pensioner's oath must be supported by the evidence of another person as to identity. The person must swear that he well knows him to be the same person described in the above affidavit. The magistrate must certify that the deponent is a person of veracity. This oath must also be authenticated by the certificate of the proper officer, under his seal of office, setting forth that the officer before whom the affidavit may be made is a Justice of the Peace, Judge, or Notary Public, as the case may be.

When a person acting as an Agent or Attorney for a Pensioner loses the certificate, the affidavit of a person is also required, which must be authenticated as above.

In every case where the Clerk of the Court, or other certifying officer, has no public seal of office, the certificate of a member of Congress, proving the official character and signature of the certifying officer, should be sent with the papers.

Mode of authenticating papers.—In every instance where the certificate of the certifying officer who authenticates the papers is not written on the same sheet which contains the affidavit, or other paper authenticated, the certificate must be attached thereto by a piece of tape or small ribbon, the ends of which must pass under the seal of office, so as to prevent any paper from being improperly attached to the certificate.

No attention will be given to persons who act as agents, unless they are known at the Department or are vouched for as respectable persons by some one who is known to the Department.

TRANSFER OF PENSIONS.

A pensioner desirous of having his pension transferred to another agency, must make his application according to the subjoined form.

The oath of the applicant must be taken before a duly qualified magistrate, whose official character and signature must be certified by the proper officer. The County Clerk, Secretary of State, or some other officer, will certify under his seal of office, that the officer who administered the oath is a justice of the peace, judge, mayor, alderman, or notary public, (as the case may be,) and that the signature purporting to be his is genuine.

The oath must be supported by the testimony of some respectable person, as to the pensioner's identity. He must swear that the person who has taken the oath is the person described in the affidavit. The magistrate must certify that the witness is a person of veracity, and the affidavit must also be authenticated in the manner above directed.

In every case where the clerk of the court, or other certifying officer, has no public seal of office, the certificate of a member of Congress, proving the official character and signature of the certifying officer, should be sent with the papers.

Form of Application for a Transfer of Pension.

STATE OF ——, } *ss.*
County of ——, }

On this ___ day of ___, 18__, before me, the subscriber, a justice of the peace for the said county of ___, personally appeared ___, who, on his oath, declares that he is the same person who formerly belonged to the company commanded by Captain ___, in the regiment commanded by Colonel ___, in the service of the United States; that his name was placed on the pension roll of the State of ___, from whence he has lately removed; that he now resides in the State [District or Territory] of ——, where he intends to remain, and wishes his pension to be there payable in future. The following are his reasons for removing from —— to ——.

(*Claimant's Signature.*)

Sworn and subscribed to before me, the day and year aforesaid.

—— *J. P.*

STATE OF ——, }
County of ——, } *ss.*
Town of ——, }

On this —— day of ——, A. D. 18—, before me, the subscriber, a —— in and for said County, duly authorized to administer oaths, personally came ——, aged —— years, and ——, aged —— years, whom I know to be residents of the County and State aforesaid, and persons whom I certify to be respectable and entitled to credit, and who being duly sworn, say that they were present and saw —— execute the foregoing affidavit by —— to the foregoing declaration, and making oath thereto in due form of law, and they further swear that they are acquainted with the said —— now present, and that he is the identical person he represents himself to be; and further, that they, deponents, do reside in the County aforesaid.

(*Witnesses' Signature.*)

Sworn to and subscribed before me, this —— day of ——, A. D. 18—, and I certify that I have no interest in this case, nor am I concerned in its prosecution.

—— *J. P.*

STATE OF ——, }
County of ——, } *ss.*

I HEREBY CERTIFY, That ——, Esq., before whom the foregoing declaration and power of attorney were made and acknowledged, and who has thereunto subscribed his name, was at the time of so doing a justice of the peace, in and for the county aforesaid, duly commissioned and sworn, and that his signature thereto is genuine.

IN TESTIMONY WHEREOF, I have hereunto set my hand and affixed the seal of —— Court, for the County aforesaid, this —— day of ——, 186–.

—— *Clerk of* ——.

POWER OF ATTORNEY TO EXAMINE PAPERS FILED IN THE PENSION OFFICE.

DEPARTMENT OF THE INTERIOR,
PENSION OFFICE, April 18, 1851.

The following rules and regulations, approved by the Secretary of the Interior, will be observed in the settlement of pension claims against the Government:

1. An agent or attorney asking to examine papers filed in any pension claim, or for the re-consideration of a claim heretofore adjudicated, must produce a power of attorney giving him the necessary authority to act as

agent of the claim, which power of attorney must be acknowledged before a justice of the peace or other person qualified to take acknowledgments or administer oaths, and must be certified under a recognized official seal. The party moreover executing such power must have taken an oath that he or she is directly interested as one of the claimants, and a certificate to that effect must accompany the power.

2. On the presentation of such authority, the Commissioner will, in his discretion, furnish an abstract of the proofs appearing in the papers filed, or permit a personal inspection of such papers.

3. Upon the presentation of the power, as required in the first rule, if it appear that the original party performing the alleged service, or his widow, is the applicant for the re-consideration of a claim heretofore adjudicated, such claim may be re-examined as a matter of right, but there shall not be more than two re-examinations without the production of further material evidence.

4. In other cases than those of the person performing service, or his widow, as prescribed in the 3d rule next preceding, no pension case which has been finally adjudicated shall be re-opened, unless on the production of satisfactory proof that the adjudication was erroneous, accompanied by an affidavit of the party applying therefor, showing that such proof has been discovered since the adjudication was made.

5. Appeals may be taken from the decision of the Commissioner of Pensions within six months from the time the decision is made and communicated to the party or his agent.

6. No application for a re-hearing will be entertained after the expiration of two years from the final adjudication of a claim and notice thereof to the applicant or his agent. After that time the party will be left to seek redress by an appeal to Congress.

J. E. HEATH,
Commissioner of Pensions.

KNOW ALL MEN BY THESE PRESENTS, That I, ——, hereby constitute and appoint ——, my true and lawful agent and attorney, to prosecute the claim of —— for any amount of —— pension, or increase of pension, that may be due; and I hereby authorize my said agent to examine all the papers and documents in relation to said claim, on file in the Departments at Washington City, or elsewhere; to file additional evidence or arguments; and to receive the certificate which may be issued for said claim, which certificate I wish made payable to ———; to appoint one or more substitutes under him for the purpose herein expressed; and to do all things that I might or could do were I personally present. Hereby ratifying and confirming all that my said attorney and agent shall lawfully do in the premises.

Witness my hand and seal, this —— day of ——, A. D. 18—.
Signed and sealed in the presence of ———

STATE OF ———, } ss.
County of ———, }

On this —— day of ——, A. D. 186 , before me, the subscriber, a Justice of the Peace in and for the County aforesaid, personally appeared ——, and acknowledged the foregoing Power of Attorney to be —— act and deed, for the purposes therein mentioned.

In testimony whereof, I hereunto set my hand, the day and year aforesaid.

——*J. P.*

I, ——, Clerk of the —— Court in the County and State aforesaid, do hereby certify that ——, before whom the foregoing papers were executed, was at the date of the same, a Justice of the Peace in and for said County, duly authorized by law to administer oaths; and the name thereunto subscribed, is —— signature.

In testimony whereof, I have hereunto subscribed my name and affixed my official seal, this —— day of ——, A. D. 186–.

——, *Clerk.*

BOUNTY MONEY AND ARREARS OF PAY.

Who are entitled to Bounty.

All volunteers who serve for a period of two years, or until the end of the war for the suppression of the rebellion, are entitled to one hundred dollars bounty, under the 5th Sec. of an act of Congress, approved July 22, 1861. (See page 33.) The heirs of all those who have volunteered for a period of two years or more, and die, or are killed in the service, are entitled to one hundred dollars bounty, and such arrears of pay as may be due the deceased at the time of his death. (See Act of July 22d, 1861, Sec. 6, page 34.)

To entitle a volunteer to draw the one hundred dollars bounty, he must serve for a period of two years, or until the end of the war. No discharged volunteer (though honorably discharged,) can receive the one hundred dollars bounty unless he shall have served for a period of two years, or until the end of the war.

All soldiers of the regular army who have enlisted since the first day of July, 1861, are entitled to the same bounties, in every respect, as those allowed, or to be allowed to the men of the volunteer forces.

The provision of law providing bounty to soldiers in the regular service is as follows:

"*And be it further enacted*, That the terms of enlistments made and to be made in the year eighteen hundred and sixty-one and eighteen hundred and sixty-two, in the regular army, including the force authorized by this act, shall be for the period of three years, and those to be made after January one, eighteen hundred and sixty-three, shall be for the term of five years, as at present authorized, and that the men enlisted in the regular forces, after the first day of July, eighteen hundred and sixty-one, shall be entitled to the same bounties, in every respect, as those allowed or to be allowed to the men of the volunteer forces." (Act of July 29th, 1861. Sec. 5.)

ARREARS OF PAY.

Discharged Soldiers.

A volunteer or soldier should receive at the time of his discharge a regular discharge, and two duplicate pay certificates, (see Form on page 89.) With these papers he can be paid by any paymaster of the army on their presentation. If the discharged volunteer or soldier has failed to obtain such certificates, and the regiment to which he belonged is disbanded or beyond his reach, or if he has obtained such certificates, and payment has for any reason been refused upon their presentation to a paymaster of the army, he should make a declaration over his signature according to Form on page 87, and forward said declaration together with his Pay Certificates and Discharge (if he has them, if not, their absence must be accounted for in said declaration) to the Second Auditor of the Treasury Department, at Washington. Such claim will be audited by the Department, and the result communicated to claimant or his Attorney.

Soldiers not entitled to Pay

The 1638th Section of the United States Army Regulations provides as follows: "In case any individual shall be discharged within three months after entering the service, for a disability which existed at that time, he shall receive neither pay nor allowances except subsistence and transportation to his home."

Soldiers not Discharged.

A volunteer or soldier at home on a furlough, or for any other cause absent from his regiment on pay day, should send power of Attorney to some member of his regiment (Captain preferred), authorizing such person to draw his pay, said power of Attorney should be as near as can be, according to Form on page 88.

Deceased Soldiers.

The heirs of a deceased volunteer or soldier are entitled to such arrears of pay as have accrued at the time of his death. Payment will be made in the following order: If the deceased was *married*—1st, To the widow; 2d, If no widow, to his child or children, (if minors, to the guardian.) If he died *unmarried*—1st, To the father; 2d, If the father is dead, to the mother; 3d, If both parents are dead, to the brothers and sisters collectively; lastly, to the heirs generally.

OFFICIAL INSTRUCTIONS OF THE SECOND AUDITOR OF THE TREASURY DEPARTMENT IN PREPARING CLAIMS FOR SOLDIER'S PAY AND BOUNTY.

To enable those who may have claims upon the United States, for money due deceased officers and soldiers, on account of services rendered, whether in the regular or volunteer service, to obtain the same, with the least delay, the following information is furnished:

Order of Payment.

Order First.—If the deceased was married, payment will be made—1st, to the widow; 2nd, If no widow, to his child, or children; (if minors, to the guardian.)

Order Second.—If he died unmarried—1st, to the father; 2nd, if the father is dead, to the mother; 3d, if both parents are dead, to the brothers and sisters collectively; lastly, to the heirs general—(to be distributed in accordance with the laws of the State in which the deceased had his domicil.)

Application, Proof and Authentication.

APPLICATION.—The claimant or claimants must make a written application, under oath, and over his, her, or their own signature stating his, her, or their name, age, residence, connection to the deceased, with the letter or name of the captain of the company and regiment to which he belonged; time of his death and the nature of the pay claimed—whether "arrears of pay," etc.; and the "$100 bounty," under Act of July 22, 1861.

PROOF.—To satisfy the accounting officers, the person or persons thus claiming is or are entitled to the money in the character he, she, or they claim, the depositions of two creditable witnesses will be required, stating that they are acquainted with the claimant or claimants, the connection held to the deceased, and that they (the deponents) are disinterested.

AUTHENTICATION.—The application and depositions above required, to be subscribed and sworn to before a judge, commissioner, notary public, or justice of the peace, duly authorized to administer oaths, accompanied by the certificate and seal of a court of record as to the fact of the said judge, etc., being duly commissioned and acting in his official capacity at the time of the execution of the foregoing papers.[1]

If the soldier *died unmarried*, it must be so stated in the application of those claiming to be his father, mother, brothers or sisters, *as well as by the witnesses.*

Proof of marriage (record evidence, if possible,) must always accompany the applications of those claiming to be the widows.

1. Papers authenticated according to the following instructions have been used successfully before the Second Auditor of the Treasury Department by the authors: "When the commission of a notary public, or a certified copy of his appointment, with his official seal and signature attached, and the certificate of the clerk of a court of the genuineness of his signature, is filed in this office, his own certificate, under his official seal, will be recognized thereafter during his term of office."

Administration.

As the taking out of "letters of administration" is attended with considerable expense, (often unnecessary,) it is suggested that it be done only when required by the Auditor.

Discharged Soldiers.

When a soldier (or volunteer) is discharged, he is (or should be) furnished with a regular "Discharge," and *two* (duplicate) "*Pay Certificates.*" Upon these papers he can be paid by a paymaster of the army upon their presentation. Should he fail to present them for payment to a paymaster, or, having presented them, and payment refused, and they are sent to this office, the applicant must state the reasons for such refusal, accompanied by proof of identity and authentication, as in the case of deceased soldiers. In no case should the "oath of identity," *on the back of the "Discharge,"* be filled up, as the "Discharge" is returned to the soldier after his claim has been acted upon. Where "Pay Certificates" have been withheld, he must send all other papers given to him at the time of his discharge.

Bounty.

No *discharged* volunteer can receive the bounty provided by the act of July 22, 1861, unless "he shall have served for a period of two years, or during the war, if sooner ended;" but "the widow, if there be one, and if not, the legal heirs of such as die, or may be killed in the service, in addition to all arrears of pay and allowances, shall receive the sum of one hundred dollars."

Pensions.

Applications for pensions on account of "disability" received in the service, should be made to the Commissioner of Pensions.

MODE OF PAYMENT.—Payments will be made by an order from the accounting officers on any paymaster of the army. Such order will require the signature of the claimant on its face before it will be paid.

Mode of Presenting Claims.

All claimants wishing to obtain information or to present claims can communicate with this office by mail, and will receive as speedy reply as the business of the office will allow.

Postage.—All communications to and from this Department will be sent free of postage. Address,

EZRA B. FRENCH,

2nd Auditor of the Tres. Dept.

Washington, D. C.

PAYMENT OF PRISONERS OF WAR.

The following General Order, issued at Washington, will be found important to those families whose husbands are now or may become prisoners of war:

[General Order No. 22.]

War Department, Adjt-Gen's Oefice
Washington, Oct. 23, 1861.

The following plan for paying to the families of officers and soldiers in the service of the United States who are or may become prisoners of war, sums due them by Government, having been approved by the President, it is published for the benefit of all concerned:

Payment will be made to persons presenting a written authority from a prisoner to draw his pay; or, without such authority, to his wife, the guardian of his minor children, or his widowed mother in the order named.

Application for such payment to be made to the senior paymaster of the district in which the prisoner is serving, and must be accompanied by the certificate of a Judge of a Court of the United States, or of some other party, under the seal of a Court of Record of the State in which the applicant is a resident, setting forth that the applicant is the wife of the prisoner, the guardian of his children, or his widowed mother, and if occupying either of the last two relationships towards him, that there is no one in existence who is more nearly related according to the above classification.

Payments will be made to parties thus authorized and identified, or their receipts made out in the manner that would be recognized by the prisoner himself, at least one month's pay being in all cases retained by the United States. The officer making the payment will see that it is entered on the last previous muster roll for the payment of the prisoner's company, or will report it, if those rolls are not in his possession, to the senior paymaster of the district, who will either attend to the entry or give notice of the payment to the Paymaster General, if the rolls have been forwarded to his office.

6

DECISIONS OF THE SECOND COMPTROLLER.

Soldier's Pay.

[The references are to volumes in the Comptroller's office.]

2. No crime except desertion forfeits the pay of a soldier, except upon sentence of a court-martial, unless, in consequence of the crime, the soldier is withdrawn from service.—*Vol.* 15, *p.* 448.

4. When a soldier, who was discharged on the expiration of his term of service, claims pay and clothing, his name not appearing on the regimental pay roll for the time embraced in his claim, the accounting officers will require the production of the descriptive certificate of his discharge, as the surest evidence that the claim has not been paid by the paymaster.

5. When the witnesses required by the regulations, to payments made to soldiers cannot be had, other satisfactory proof of the signature may be received.—*Vol.* 14, *p* 50.

6. A receipt by mark, witnessed by two paymasters' clerks, is a substantial compliance with the regulation.—*Vol.* 14, *p.* 75.

7. When a soldier is discharged, and his account settled and paid by a paymaster, the payment purporting to be in full, that payment is to be considered final, unless shown by conclusive testimony to have been erroneous.—*Jno. A. Powell's case, January*, 1848.

8. When, from the situation of his company, or the nature of the service, a soldier cannot receive his discharge when his term expires, and is from necessity retained in service, he is to be paid up to the time of his actual discharge.—*Vol.* 6, *p.* 149.

9. A soldier discharged on habeas corpus as a minor, forfeits all pay and allowances previously due, both by the Regulations of the Army, and general principles.—*Vol.* 15, *p.* 38.

10. When an officer or soldier is furloughed, in anticipation of his discharge or the expiration of his term of service, he cannot claim for the balance of his term both his travel pay and his pay as in service.—*Lieut. Fellnagle's case, and W. S. Thompson's case, Oct.* 19, 1848.

11. A soldier, who is taken prisoner by the enemy, is entitled to his pay and allowance during the time he is detained, and to travelling allowance from the place where he is released to his home. Volunteers however, are not, under such circumstances, entitled to compensation for use and risk of horses.—*Vol.* 12, *p.* 429.

12. A private soldier of militia or volunteers, who is illegally and against his will discharged from service, is entitled to his pay up to the time of the discharge of the company to which he belonged, or to the expiration of his term of enlistment.—*W. C. Hayse's case, June* 16, 1849.

13. A soldier under arrest by the civil authority or a criminal charge, will be entitled to his pay for the time he was in custody, provided he is tried and acquitted, or discharged without trial.—*Case of Dennes Clary, Jan.* 8, 1844.

Deceased Claimants.

1. In order to show that the person claiming money due a deceased person from the United States, has a legal right to receive it, he should produce and file with the disbursing officer making the payments, the original letter of administration, or a copy thereof duly certified, or an official certificate from the clerk of the court from which it issued, that it appears by the records of said court that he has been duly appointed, and is legally empowered to act as administrator on the deceased person's estate.—*Vol.* 12, *p.* 184.

2. Where the balance due a deceased person is paid to an administrator deriving his authority from a court of competent jurisdiction, though obtained by fraudulent means, payment will not be made again when claimed by the true representative of the deceased. But where payment is made to an administrator whose authority is derived from a court possessing no power to grant administration, the legal representatives of the deceased have a valid claim on the government for the money. When the jurisdiction of the court granting the power is denied, and the question is one of fact merely, such as the residence of the deceased, etc., the most conclusive evidence of the want of jurisdiction will be required.—*Philip Robinson's case*, *April* 10, 1851.

3. In the case of a gratuity granted by act of Congress to the relatives of deceased persons, the collateral relatives, whether of the whole or half blood, should participate equally, in the order pointed out in the act.—*Dec. Sec. Compt.*, *Nov.* 19, 1830.

4. When the amount due from the United States to a deceased person has been paid to one claiming to be the only brother of the deceased, upon proof that was then deemed satisfactory that he was the only brother, and that there was no widow, and other claim for the money is presented by a person claiming to be the widow, the clearest evidence should be required of the fraud and perjury of the proof on which payment was made, of the absence of all knowledge of it on the part of the second claimant, and of her right as the widow, before the money is paid again.—*Vol.* 15, *pp.* 11, 173.

5. Questions as to the right of the whole or half blood to inherit balances due deceased persons, will be determined in conformity with the law of the State of which the deceased was a citizen.—*Sergeant W. C. Baker's case*, 22*d September*, 1849.

6. The government do not recognize an administrator appointed without the consent of the heirs of the deceased.—*Vol.* 3, *p.* 37.

7. Where arrearages are claimed by an executor, for the benefit of others, either the will should be probated in the county where the deceased lived, or those interested in the trust should signify their assent that the amount should be paid to the executor without probate of the will.—*Vol.* 15, *p.* 73.

8. Payment of an amount due a deceased person for articles purchased by the Navy Department, may be made to the guardian of the children of the deceased, where it appears by the certificate of the probate court, that the wards of the guardian are the sole heirs, and also that the debts of the deceased have been paid, and the estate

closed by a settlement of the administrator's account; otherwise payment should be made to the administrator.—*Vol.* 14, *p.* 206.

9. Arrears due a deceased soldier may be paid without administration to the widow, child, father, mother, brothers, and sisters, but not to more remote heirs; and no after application for the benefit of creditors will be recognized.

10. Arrears of pay may be legally paid to the mother of a deceased soldier, he being an illegitimate son, leaving neither wife or child.

11. A. soldier cannot, by a will, transfer his right to extra pay or land; but *can* his arrears of pay.

Widow's Declaration for Bounty Money and Arrears.

STATE OF ——, }
County of ——; } *ss.*

On this —— day of —— 186 , before me, a —— in and for the County and State above named, personally appeared [1]—— who, after being duly sworn according to law, declares and says —— that she is aged —— years, that she is a resident of ——, County of ——, State of ——, and that she is the widow of [2]—— who was a [3]—— in Company [4]—— commanded by Captain —— of the —— Regiment of —— Volunteers, commanded by Colonel ——, and who —— at —— on or about the —— day of —— 186 , while in the service of the United States.

That she was married to the said [2]—— on the —— day of —— 186 , at —— by one —— a —— that her name before her said marriage was ——, and that she has remained a widow since the death of her said husband. And she further states that she believes there is —— public record of her said marriage [5]——

She makes this declaration for the purpose of obtaining the Bounty Money, Arrears of Pay, and all other arrearages or sums of money due her by reason of the services of the soldier above named, under and by virtue of An Act of Congress, passed July 22, A. D. 1861, granting to the widow, if there be one, if not, to the legal heirs of such as die or may be killed in the service, in addition to all arrears of pay and allowances, the sum of one hundred dollars; also, of all other acts now in force upon this subject. And she hereby constitutes and appoints ——, her Attorney in fact, to prosecute this claim, and authorizes him to receive and receipt for a draft or certificate, for the amount that may be allowed her.

(*Claimant's Signature.*)

Sworn to and subscribed before me, the day and year first above written, and on the same day personally came —— and —— residents of —— in the County of —— State aforesaid, who, being duly sworn according to law, declare that they are personally acquainted with Mrs.[1] —— widow of [2]—— who has made and subscribed the foregoing declaration, and were acquainted with her and her said husband before he entered the service, and know that they lived together as man and wife, and were so reputed. That she is the widow of the identical [2]—— who performed the military service mentioned in said declaration, and has remained a widow since his death. That their knowledge of the identity of her husband with the soldier is derived from [7]——

And they further testify that they reside as above stated, and are disinterested in this claim.

(*Witnesses' Signatures.*)

Sworn to and subscribed before me, and I certify that I am not interested in this claim, or concerned in its prosecution; that I believe the affiants to be credible persons, and the declarant the person she represents —— to be.

Magistrate's Signature.)

STATE OF ——, } *ss.*
County of——, }

I, ——, Clerk of the County Court in and for the County and State above named, do hereby certify that —— Esq., before whom the foregoing declaration and affidavits were made, and who has thereunto signed his name, twas, at the time of so doing, an acting ____ , in and for the County and State above named, duly commissioned and sworn, that all his official acts, as such, are entitled to full faith and credit, and that his signature thereto is genuine.

IN TESTIMONY WHEREOF, I have hereunto set my hand affixed the seal of said Court, at —— in said County, this —— day of —— A. D. 186 .

—— *Clerk.*

1. Claimant's name.
2. Soldier's name.
3. Soldier's rank.
4. Alphabetical title of Company.
5. PROOF OF MARRIAGE.—If there is a County, Town or Church record of the marriage, a duly certified copy of such record must be sent. If there is no public, but a private or family record containing the marriage or the births of children, such private record should be sent. It will be returned when used. Parol evidence of the marriage is not admissible until the absence of record evidence is accounted for. If the testimony of persons who were present at the marriage can be produced, it should be sent; and if such testimony cannot be had, the declarant will so state. Testimony to cohabitation and general repute as man and wife will not alone be sufficient proof of the marriage, unless the claimant *is unable to present either public or private record evidence, or the testimony of persons who were present, and so states in her declaration.*
7. Witnesses will here state in what manner they derive their knowledge of the soldier's identity, and if they or either of them were present at the marriage, it should be here stated.

Claim of Heirs for Arrears, Bounty Money, &c., of Deceased Officer or Soldier.

STATE OF ——, } *ss.*
County of——, }

On this —— day of —— 186–, before me, a ——, in and for the County and State above named, personally appeared [1]—— aged —— years, a resident of ——, County of ——, State of —— who being duly sworn according to law, declare that [2]—— he —— the [3]——

and heir of [4]—— who was a —— of Company [5]——, commanded by Captain —— in the —— Regiment of —— Volunteers. That the said —— volunteered at —— on or about the —— day of —— 186–, for —— and —— at —— on or about the —— day of —— 186 , while in said service. That the said —— left surviving him no widow, or child, or children[6]——

This declaration is made for the purpose of obtaining the Arrears of Pay, Bounty Money, Extra Pay, and all other arrearages or sums of money due by reason of the services of the soldier above named; and ——— is hereby constituted ——— Attorney to prosecute this claim, and is authorized to receive and receipt for a draft payable to the order of this declarant or declarants for whatever sum may be allowed on the same, and to assign and convert the same into current funds.

(Signature of Heirs.)

Sworn to and subscribed before me, the day and year first above written, and on the same day personally appeared —— and —— residents of —— who being duly sworn according to law, declare that they are personally acquainted with ——— who has made and subscribed the foregoing declaration, and know that —— he —— the —— and heir-at-law of —— who was a —— in Captain —— Company —— of the —— Regiment of —— Volunteers, and who died or was killed while in the service of the United States, as stated in said declaration. That the said ——— left surviving him no widow, or child, or children —— That their knowledge of —— identity as heir of the soldier named is derived from .... That they reside as above stated, and are disinterested in this claim.

(Witnesses' Signatures.)

Sworn to and subscribed before me, and I certify that I am not interested in this claim, or concerned in its prosecution; and I believe the affiants to be credible persons, and the declarant the person he represent —— to be.

———

STATE OF ———, }
County of ———, } *ss.*

I, ———, Clerk of the County Court in and for the County and State above named, do hereby certify that ——— Esq., before whom the foregoing affidavits were made, and who has thereunto signed his name, was, at the time of so doing a ———— in and for the County and State above named, duly commissioned and sworn, that all his official acts, as such, are entitled to full faith and credit, and that his signature thereto is genuine.

In Testimony Whereof, I have hereunto signed my name, and affixed my official seal, this —— day of —— A. D. 186 .

Clerk of the County Court of —— County.

Claims are paid in the following order: If the deceased was *married*—1st, To the widow; 2d, If no widow, to his child or children (if minors, to the guardian). If he died *unmarried*—1st, To the father; 2d, If the father is dead, to the mother; 3d, If both parents are dead, to the brothers and sisters collectively; lastly, to the heirs generally.

When there are several heirs, and it will be difficult to have them unite in a declaration, one of them should take out letters of administration, and make the claim as administrator. In such cases, the names of all the heirs must be stated in the declaration and affidavit, and the administration bond be not less than double the amount of the claim.

NOTES—1. Claimant or claimants' name, age and residence.
2. *He*, or *she is*, or *they are*.
3. Claimant's connection to the deceased; *father*, *mother*, or as the case may be.
4. Soldier's name.
5. Alphabetical title of the Company.
6. If the claim is not by the father, it must be expressed here that there are surviving no heirs who would be entitled under the order of payment in preference to the claimant; thus, if a brother and sister claim, add: "*or father or mother, and no brothers or sisters other than these* (or *the above*) *declarants*."

Application of Soldiers for Arrears of Pay, or for Arrears of Pay and Bounty.

STATE OF ____, }
County of ____, } *ss.*

On this ____ day of ____, 186—, before me, a ____ in and for the county and State above named, and by law duly authorized to administer oaths for general purposes, personally appeared ____, aged ____ years, who being duly sworn according to law, declares that he is not indebted or accountable to the United States on any account whatever; and he further states that he is the identical ____ who was a ____ in Company ____, commanded by Captain ____, in the ____ Regiment of ____ Volunteers, commanded by Colonel ____; that he enlisted at ____, in the State of ____ on or about the ____ day of ____ 18—, for the term of ____, and was honorably discharged at ____ on or about the ____ day of ____, 18—, by reason of ____; and that he claims there is due him from the United States, for pay and allowances, as follows:

He makes this declaration to obtain the arrears of pay, bounty money, extra pay, and all other arrearages or sums of money due him by reason of the services above named; and he hereby constitutes and appoints ____, his attorney, to prosecute this claim, and authorises him to receive and receipt for a certificate for whatever sum may be allowed on the same, and to attend to and procure the settlement of such business as deponent may have with the United States, in any office or department of the same, and to receive and receipt for all sums of money that may be found due deponent, upon any account or claim now unsettled.

(*Signature of Claimant.*)

Sworn to and subscribed, and acknowledged before me, the day and year first above mentioned, and on the same day personally came before me ____ and ____ residents of ____, to me known as credible witnesses, who being duly sworn according to law, declare that they are personally acquainted with ____ who has made and subscribed the foregoing declaration, and know that he is the identical person who performed the service therein named; that their knowledge of his identity is derived from ____. That they are disinterested in the claim, and reside at the place above named.

(*Signature of Witnesses.*)

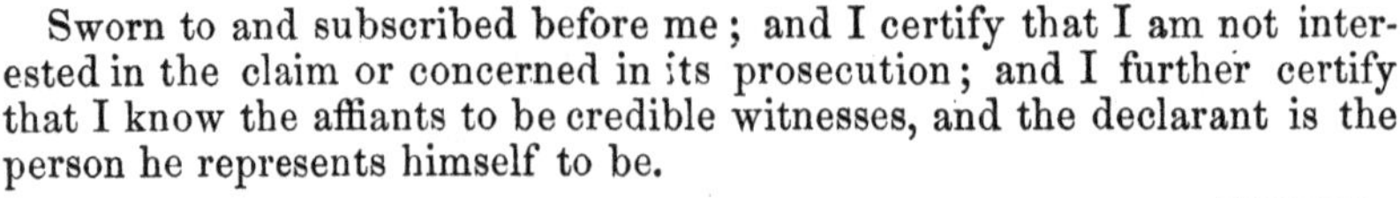

Sworn to and subscribed before me; and I certify that I am not interested in the claim or concerned in its prosecution; and I further certify that I know the affiants to be credible witnesses, and the declarant is the person he represents himself to be.

———

STATE OF ——, }
County of ——, } *ss.*

I, ____, Clerk of the County Court in and for the County and State above named, do hereby certify that ____, Esq., before whom the forgoing affidavits were made, and who has thereunto signed his name, was at the time of so doing a ____, in and for the county and State above named, duly commissioned and sworn, that all his official acts as such are entitled to full faith and credit, and that his signature thereto is genuine.

In testimony whereof, I have hereunto signed my name and affixed my official seal this ____ day of ____ 186—.

——, *Clerk.*

Power of Attorney for Drawing Soldier's Pay.

KNOW ALL MEN BY THESE PRESENTS: That I, ____, a, ____ in Company ____, commanded by Captain ____, of the ____ Regiment of ____ Volunteers, commanded by Colonel ____, do hereby make, constitute and ____, of ____ my true and lawful attorney, for me and in my name, place and stead, to ask, demand, receive and receipt for any and all pay and money due me from the United States Government, for services in said company. And I do hereby authorize my said attorney, for me, to sign the pay roll of said regiment and perform any and all other acts necessary to be done in the premises as fully, to all intents and purposes, as I, myself, if personally present, could do, thereby ratifying all that my said attorney shall or may do in the premises.

Signed, sealed and delivered this ____ day of ____ }
186 , in presence of ____. }

(*Seal.*)

STATE OF ——, }
County of ——, } *ss.*

I, the undersigned, a ____, in and for the county and State aforesaid, do hereby certify that on this ____ day of ____, 18—, appeared ____, who is personally known to me to be the same person whose name is subscribed to the within power of attorney as a party thereto and acknowledged the same to be his act and deed for the purposes therein mentioned. I also certify that he is the identical ____, who performed the military service referred to in the above power of attorney.

In testimony whereof witness my hand and official seal the date above written.

————.

Certificates to be given a Soldier at the time of his Discharge.

(*Army Regulations page* 360.)

I certify that the within named ____, a ____ of Captain ____ Company (____), of the ____ regiment of ____, born in ____, in the State of ____, aged ____ years, ____ feet __ inches high, ____ complexion, ____ eyes, ____ hair, and by profession a ____, was enlisted by ____, at ____, on the ____ day of ____, eighteen hundred and ____, to serve for ____ years, and is now entitled to a discharge by reason of ____.

The said ____ was last paid by Paymaster ____, to include the ____ day of ____, eighteen hundred and ____, and has pay due him from that time to the present date.

There is due to him ____ dollars retained pay.

There is due to him ____ dollars on account of clothing not drawn in kind.

He is indebted to the United States ____ dollars, on account of extra clothing, etc.

He is indebted to ____, laundress at ____, ____ dollars.

The contract price of the rations at ____ is ____ cents.

Given in duplicate at ____, this ____ day of ____, 18__.

______ *Commanding Company.*

A discharged volunteer should present his discharge with this certificate, signed in duplicate by his Captain, to any United States Paymaster, who will thereupon adjust and pay his account.

DECEASED OFFICERS' EFFECTS.

Whenever an officer dies, or is killed at any military post or station, or in the vicinity of the same, it will be the duty of the commanding officer to report the fact direct to the Adjutant-General, with the date, and any other information proper to be communicated. If an officer die at a distance from a military post, any officer having intelligence of the same will in like manner communicate it, specifying the day of his decease; a duplicate of the report will be sent to Department Head-Quarters.

Inventories of the effects of deceased officers, required by the 94th Article of War, will be transmitted to the Adjutant-General. If a legal administrator or family connection be present, and take charge of the effects, it will be so stated to the Adjutant-General.

DECEASED SOLDIERS.

Inventories of the effects of deceased non-commissioned officers and soldiers, required by the 95th Article of War, will be forwarded to the Adjutant-General, by the commander of the company to which the deceased belonged, and a duplicate of the same to the Colonel of the regiment. Final statements of pay, clothing, etc., will be sent with the inventories. When a soldier dies at a post or station, absent from his company, it will be the duty of his immediate commander to furnish the required inventory, and, at the same time, to forward to the commanding officer of the company to which the soldier belonged, a report of his death, specifying the date, place, and cause; to what time he was last paid, and the money or other effects in his possession at the time of his decease; which report will be noted on the next muster-roll of the company to which the man belonged. Each inventory will be endorsed, "Inventory of the effects of ____ ____, late of company (____) ____ regiment of ____, who died at ____, the ____ day of ____, 186__."

If a legal representative receive the effects, it will be stated in the report. If the soldier leave no effects, the fact will be reported.

Should the effects of a deceased non-commissioned officer or soldier not be administered upon within a short period after his decease, they shall be disposed of by a Council of Administration, under the authority of the commanding officer of the post, and the proceeds deposited with the Paymaster, to the credit of the United States, until they shall be claimed by the legal representatives of the deceased.

In all such cases of sales by the Council of Administration, a statement in detail, or account of the proceeds, duly certified by the Council and commanding officer, accompanied by the Paymaster's receipt for the proceeds, will be forwarded by the commanding officer to the Adjutant General. The statement will be endorsed: "Report of the proceeds of the effects of ____ ____, late of Company (____), ____ regiment of ____, who died at ____, the ____ day of ____, 186 ."

Regulations in regard to Sutlers.

(Army Regulations, Article XXV.)

No Sutler shall sell to an enlisted man on credit to a sum exceeding *one-third* of his monthly pay, *within the same month*, without the written sanction of the company commander, or the commanding officer of the post or station, if the man does not belong to a company; and not exceeding *one-half* of the monthly pay with such permission.

Three days before the last of every month the Sutler shall render, for verification, to the company commander, or to the commanding officer, as the case may be, according to the meaning of the preceding paragraph, a written and separate account in each case of any charges he may have against enlisted men for collection, and the officer shall submit the account to the soldier for acknowledgment and signature, and witness the same. In case of death, desertion, or removal from the post (of the soldier,) the account will be rendered immediately. If the soldier dispute the account and the Sutler insist, and in the case of death and desertion, the Sutler will be required to establish the account by affidavit indorsed on it before any officer authorized to administer an oath. Debts thus verified as due the Sutler are to be noted on the muster rolls, and will be paid by the Paymaster out of the arrearages due to the soldier at the time of death, desertion, discharge, or sentence of court-martial; the sums due the Government and laundress being first paid. Every facility will be afforded to the Sutler in the collection of the just debts contracted with him. He will, to this end, be allowed to take his place at the pay-table with his books and accounts.

Sutlers shall not farm-out or underlet the business and privileges granted by their appointment.

HORSES AND OTHER PROPERTY, LOST OR DESTROYED.

AN ACT to provide for the payment of horses and other property lost or destroyed in the military service of the United States, approved March 3d, 1849.

Be it enacted by the Senate and House of Representatives of the United States of America in Congress assembled, That any field, or staff, or other officer, mounted militiaman, volunteer, ranger, or cavalry, engaged in the military service of the United States since the 18th of June, 1812, or who shall hereafter be in said service, and has sustained, or shall sustain damage without any fault or negligence on his part, while in said service, by the loss of a horse in battle, or by the loss of a horse wounded in battle, and which has died, or shall die, of said wound, or, being so wounded, shall be abandoned by order of his officer and lost, or shall sustain damage by the loss of any horse by death or abandonment, because of the unavoidable dangers of the sea when on board a United States transport-vessel, or because the United States failed to supply transportation for the horse, and the owner was compelled by the order of his commanding officer to embark and leave him, or in consequence of the United States failing to supply sufficient forage, or because the rider was dismounted and separated from his horse, and ordered to do duty on foot, at a station detached from his horse, and when the officer in the immediate command ordered or shall order the horse turned out to graze in the woods, prairies, or commons, because the United States failed, or shall fail, to supply sufficient forage, and the loss was or shall be consequent thereof, or for the loss of necessary equipage in consequence of the loss of his horse as aforesaid, shall be allowed and paid the value thereof, not to exceed two hundred dollars; provided, that if any payment has been or shall be made to any one aforesaid for the use and risk, or for forage after the death, loss, or abandonment of his horse, said payment shall be deducted from the value thereof, unless he satisfied or shall satisfy the paymaster at the time he made or shall make the payment, or thereafter show by proof that he was remounted, in which case the deduction shall only extend to the time he was on foot; and provided, also, if any payment shall have been or shall hereafter be made to any person above mentioned on account of clothing, to which he was not entitled by law, such payment shall be deducted from the value of his horse or accoutrements.

SEC. 2. *And be it further enacted,* That any person who has sustained or shall sustain damage by the capture or destruction by an enemy, or by the abandonment or destruction, by the order of the commanding general, the commanding officer, or quartermaster, of any horse, mule, ox, wagon, cart, boat, sleigh, or harness, while such property was in the military service of the United States, either by impressment or contract, except in cases where the risk to which the property would be exposed was agreed to be incurred by the owner, and any person who has sustained or shall sustain damage by the death or abandonment and loss of any such horse, mule, or ox, while in the service aforesaid, in consequence of the failure on the part of the United States to furnish the same with sufficient forage; and any person who has lost, or shall lose, or has had or shall have destroyed by unavoidable accident any horse, mule, ox, wagon, cart, boat, sleigh, or harness, while such property was in the service aforesaid, shall be allowed and paid the value thereof at the time he entered the service: *Provided*, it shall appear that such loss, capture, abandonment, destruction, or death, was without any fault or negligence on the part of the owner of the property, and while it was actually employed in the service of the United States.

SEC. 3. *And be it further enacted*, That the claims provided for under this act shall be adjusted by the Third Auditor, under such rules as shall be prescribed by the Secretary of War, under the direction or with the assent of the President of the United States, as well in regard to the receipt of applications of claimants as the species and degree of evidence, the manner in which such evidence shall be taken and authenticated, which rules shall be such as in the opinion of the President shall be best calculated to obtain the object of this act, paying a due regard as well to the claims of individual justice as to the interest of the United States; which rules and regulations shall be published for four weeks in such newspapers, in which the laws of the United States are published, as the Secretary of War shall direct.

SEC. 4. *And be it further enacted*, That in all adjudications of said Auditor upon the claims above-mentioned, whether such judgments be in favor of or adverse to the claim, shall be entered in a book provided by him for that purpose and under his direction; and when such judgments shall be in favor of such claim, the claimant, or his legal representative, shall be entitled to the amount thereof, certified by said Auditor, at the Treasury of the United States.

SEC. 5. *And be it further enacted*, That in all instances where any minor has been or shall be engaged in the military service of the United States, and was or shall be provided with a horse or equipments, or military accoutrements, by his parent or guardian, and has died, or shall die, without paying for said property, and the same has been or shall be lost, captured, destroyed, or abandoned, in the manner before mentioned, said parent or guardian shall be allowed pay therefor on making satisfactory proof as in other cases, and the further proof that he is entitled thereto by having furnished the same.

SEC. 6. *And be it further enacted*, That in all instances where any person, other than a minor, has been or shall be engaged in the military service aforesaid, and has been or shall be provided with a horse or equipments, or with military accoutrements, by any person, the owner thereof, who has risked or shall take the risk of such horse, equipments, or military accoutrements on himself, and the same has been or shall be lost, captured, destroyed, or abandoned in the manner before mentioned, such owner shall be allowed pay therefor, on making proof, as in other cases, and the further proof that he is entitled thereto by having furnished the same and having taken the risk on himself.

SEC. 7. *And be it further enacted*, That in all cases where horses have been condemned by a board of officers on account of their unfitness for service, in consequence of the government failing to supply forage, all such horses and their equipage shall be allowed and paid for, whenever the facts shall be proven, by legal and satisfactory evidence, whether oral or written, that such condemned horse and the equipage was turned over to a quartermaster of the army, whether any receipt therefor was given and produced or not.

RULES AND REGULATIONS.

Under the 3d section of the act, the Secretary of War, with the approval of the President, on the 26th of March, 1849, prescribed certain rules and regulations under which the claims were to be adjusted by the Third Auditor. They are substantially as follows:

Claims under the act, are divided into *three* classes, viz:

Those under the 1st section being the *first* class,

Those under the 2d, 5th and 6th sections, being the *second* class,

Those under the 7th section being the *third* class.

All claims to be presented to the office of the Third Auditor of the Treasury, and substantiated by such evidence as is hereinafter designated with respect to cases of the class under which it falls.

First Class of Cases.

To establish a claim under the provision of the 1st section of the act, the claimant must adduce the evidence of the officer under whose command he served when the loss occurred, if alive: or if dead, then of the next surviving officer, describing the property, the value thereof, at the time of entering the service, the time and manner in which the loss happened, and whether or not it was sustained without any fault or negligence on the claimant's part. The evidence should also, in case the claimant was remounted after the loss, state when remounted, how long he continued so, and explain whether the horse whereon he was remounted had not been furnished by the United States, or been owned by another mounted militiaman or volunteer to whom payment for the use and risk thereof, or for its forage, whilst in the possession of the claimant, may have been made; and if it had been thus owned, should name the person and the command to which he belonged. And in every instance in which the claim may extend to equipage, the several articles of which the same consisted and separate value of each should be specified.

Second Class of Cases.

To establish a claim under the provisions of the 2d, 5th, and 6th sections of the act, it will, in addition to the testimony required under the head of First Class of Cases, be necessary, in cases where the property lost was in the service by contract or impressment, to produce the testimony of the officer or agent of the United States who impressed or contracted for the service of the property mentioned in such claim, and also of the officer under whose command the same was employed at the time of the capture, destruction, loss or abandonment, declaring in what way the property was taken into the service of the United States, the value thereof, whether or not the risk to which it would be exposed was agreed to be incurred by the owner; and whether or not, as regarded horses, mules, oxen, he engaged to supply the same with sufficient forage, in what manner the loss happened, and whether or not it was sustained without any fault or negligence on his part.

A parent or guardian of a deceased minor will, in addition to such testimony applicable to his claim as is previously described, have to furnish proof, that he provided the minor with the property therein mentioned, that the minor died without paying for such property, and that he, the parent or guardian is entitled to payment for it by his having furnished the same.

Sec. 6. Besides the testimony in support of his claim hereinbefore required, every such owner thereof will have to prove that he did provide the horse, equipments or military accoutrements therein mentioned, and took the risk thereof on himself, and that he is entitled to pay therefor, by having furnished the same and taking the risk thereof on himself, and this proof should be contained in a deposition of the person who had been so provided by him with such horse, equipments or military accoutrements.

Third Class of Cases.

To establish a claim under the provisions of the 7th section of the act, the claimant must adduce the evidence of the witnesses mentioned under the head of First Class of Cases, satisfactorily proving that the property therein described was, while in the military service of the United States, condemned by a board of officers on account of their being rendered unfit for service in consequence of the Government failing to supply forage, and that such property was turned over to a quartermaster of the United States army, explaining when the claimant was remounted, etc., as required in said first class of cases.

In no case can the production of evidence previously described be dispensed with, unless the impracticability of producing it be clearly proved, and then the nearest and best other evidence of which the case is susceptible must be furnished in lieu thereof.

Every claim must be accompanied by a deposition of the claimant "declaring that he has not received from any officer or agent of the United States any horse or horses, equipage, accoutrements, mule wagon, cart, boat, sleigh or harness, (as the case may be), in lieu of the property lost, nor any compensation for the same," and be supported, if practicable, by the original valuation list, if made by the appraisers of the property at the time the same was taken into the United States service, and in cases where the loss is alleged to have occurred because the United States failed to supply transportation for the horse, and the owner was compelled by the order of his commanding officer to embark and leave him, as provided for in the first section of the law; the affidavit of the claimant must, in addition to the declaration above mentioned, declare "that he did, in obedience to the order of his officer, leave said horse or equipage, and that he never sold or otherwise disposed of said horse or equipage, and never received any compensation for said horse or equipage from any person whatever."

All evidence, other than the certificates of officers who at the time of giving them were in the military service of the United States, must be sworn to before some judge, justice of the peace, or other person duly authorized to administer oaths, and of which authority proof should accompany the evidence.

Form of Application.

STATE OF —— } ss.
County of —— }

On this —— day of——, A. D. 18—, personally appeared before the subscriber, a Justice of the Peace, duly authorized by law to administer oaths in and for said county ——, who is to me personally well known as a resident of ——, in the State of ——, and who, being by me duly sworn, deposes and says, that he is the identical ——, who was a ——, in the company commanded by ——, in the regiment of ——, commanded by ——, that he entered the service of the United States on or about the ——, day of ——, A. D., 18—, and was regularly mustered into said service, and mounted upon a horse of the following description, viz.:———., which said horse was appraised in due form of the value of $——, that he continued mounted upon the said horse until the —— day of ——, 18—, when the said horse was lost in consequence of, and in the manner following, viz.: ———That at the time of the loss aforesaid he was under the immediate command of ——, that he was remounted on the —— day of ——, A. D. 18—, on a horse valued at $——, which he obtained of ——, who was ——, and continued so remounted until the —— day of 18—, when he was regularly and honorably mustered out of the service by ——.

And further, that he has not received from any officer or agent of the United States any horse, or other property in lieu of the horse lost as aforesaid, nor has he received any compensation for the same; the same having been lost without any fault or negligence on his part.

SWORN TO AND SUBSCRIBED, before me, this } (*Claimant's Sig.*)
—— day of ——, A. D. 18—. }

————,*J. P.*

STATE OF —— } ss.
County of —— }

On this —— day of ——, A. D., 18—, personally appeared before me, the subscriber, a Justice of the Peace, duly authorized by law to administer oaths, in and for the said county ——, who is to me personally well known as a resident of said county, and a credible witness: who, being by me duly sworn, deposes and says, that he is the identical ——, who was the *Captain* commanding a company of ——, in the Regiment commanded by Col. ——, in the service of the United States, in the war with ——, that —— was a ——, in the said company, having been regularly enrolled and mustered into the service, that at the time of his muster he was mounted on a horse of the following description, viz. :———, which said horse was duly appraised and valued at the sum of $——, that the horse above described was lost, on the —— day of ——, in consequence of ——, in the manner following, viz :——, which said loss was sustained without any fault or negligence on the part of the claimant———.

And deponent further states, that the said —— was remounted after said loss, on the —— day of ——, A. D. 18—, and continued so remounted until the —— day of ——, A. D. 18—.

And deponent further states, that the horse upon which the said —— was remounted as aforesaid, was not furnished by the United States, or any of their officers or agents, or been owned by another mounted militiaman or volunteer, to whom payment for the loss and risk thereof, or for its forage, while in possession of the said ——, could have been made, *except* ———.

And deponent further states, that the horse upon which the said ——, was remounted, was purchased by him of one ——, and the sum of $—— paid for the same.

And deponent further states, that the said —— was honorably discharged on the —— day of —— A. D. 18—.

SUBSCRIBED AND SWORN TO, before me, this —— day of ——, A. D. 18— } ———

——*J. P.*

KNOW ALL MEN BY THESE PRESENTS, that I, ——, of —— named in the foregoing declaration and affidavit, do thereby constitute and appoint—— my true and lawful attorney, authorizing him to file this my claim for payment for a horse lost in the military service of the United States, and to do all acts, necessary and proper in the premises; to receive and receipt for a draft payable to my order for such sum as may be found due upon examination and settlement of my claim.

WITNESS my hand and seal this —— day of ——, A. D. 18—

Signed, sealed in presence of —— [SEAL.]

STATE OF ———, }
County of———, } *ss.*

On this —— day of —— 186 , personally appeared before me the above named ——, to me known, and acknowledged the foregoing Power of Attorney to be his act and deed for the purpose therein mentioned.

—— *J. P.*

STATE OF ———, }
County of———, } *ss.*

I HEREBY CERTIFY, that ——, Esquire, before whom the foregoing Power of Attorney has been acknowledged, and who has thereunto subscribed his name, was, at the time of such acknowledgment, a Justice of the Peace, in and for the said County and State, duly commissioned and sworn, and authorized by law to take the same.

IN TESTIMONY WHEREOF, I have hereunto set my hand and affixed the seal of —— County Court, (a Court of record), this —— day of ——, 18—

—— *Clerk.*

BROTHERTON & NETTELTON,

BANKERS,

47 CLARK STREET,

CHICAGO, - - - - - - - ILLINOIS.

DEALERS IN

COIN, EXCHANGE, UNCURRENT MONEY,

AND

GOVERNMENT SECURITIES.

E. G. L. FAXON,

IMPORTER AND MANUFACTURER OF

PAPER HANGINGS!

CURTAIN PAPERS,

WINDOW SHADES, ETC.

Keeping always on hand a full and complete assortment of everything in the line, and selling exclusive for CASH, I can offer superior inducements to any house West, and compete successfully with Eastern Manufacturers.

ORDERS PROMPTLY ATTENDED TO.

ALSO, MANUFACTURER OF

BEDDING OF EVERY DESCRIPTION!

SPRING, CURLED HAIR, COTTON, "EXCELSIOR," SEA GRASS AND HUSK MATTRESSES; FEATHER BEDS, BOLSTERS, PILLOWS, COMFORTERS, BLANKETS, SHEETS, PILLOW SLIPS, SPREADS, ETC., ALWAYS ON HAND OR MADE TO ORDER.

PARTICULAR ATTENTION CALLED TO MY

PORTABLE SPRING MATTRESS,

MADE TO ORDER, TO FIT ALL STYLES OF BEDSTEADS. IT IS THE BEST AND MOST DURABLE BED EVER USED. CAN BE CLEANED WITHOUT TAKING FROM THE BEDSTEAD.

☞ Also, to my STEAM CURED FEATHERS, free from the smell of the quill, so offensive in "Live Geese" Feathers. The only place in the North-west where these can be procured.

☞ PARTICULAR ATTENTION PAID TO ORDERS. ☜

E. G. L. FAXON,

P. O. Box 2616. 70 Lake Street.

PEOPLE'S PENSION & BOUNTY MONEY OFFICE.

SNYDER, COOK & CO.,

CHICAGO, ILL.,

95 Lake Street, Corner of Dearborn, Rooms 12 and 13,

Attorneys for War Claimants

. IN EVERY STATE IN THE UNION.

We devote our *entire attention* to the prosecution of Claims against the Government.

No Business of any other kind, character or nature whatever, whether local or general, will be transacted at our offices.

Preparing, Corresponding and Paying Over Office, Chicago, Ill. Collection Office, Washington, D. C.

All correspondence in regard to claims, and all claims when authenticated, and all communications from agents, must be addressed to us at Chicago, Illinois.

One agent will be given employment by us in every County in the United States, where there is none already employed. Application for such vacant agencies solicited, but applicants must be men of integrity, as moneys pass through their hands when collected.

Parties having Government Claims to collect in any part of the United States, where we have no local agents will write directly to us at Chicago, Illinois. Their moneys will be promptly collected and immediately paid over.

We employ no outside agent or attorney at Washington, but do the whole work of Receiving, Preparing and Prosecuting Claims all within our own firm, hence our clients have to pay but *one fee*, and that about one-half the amount that has commonly been charged claimants heretofore. As our increasing business demands it, our senior partner at Washington will shortly open an office there, parties may then address us at Washington, D. C., or Chicago, Ill. To Agents, we say take no agency until you know your principals are men of worth and integrity. To war claimants we say, employ no local attorney, or any advertised firm in Washington City, or elsewhere, until you write and find out that those you employ have facilities for making your collections in some *reasonable* time, and sufficient integrity to pay over immediately when collected.

Address

SNYDER, COOK & CO.,

CHICAGO, ILL.

Refer to TRIBUNE COMAANY,
BRADNER, SMITH & CO.,
G. W. CUSHMAN & CO.,
HON. E. P. PERRY,
} Chicago, Ill.

☞Employ no parties who advertise for outside business.☜

A. B. ROFF,

Attorney at Law and Land Agent,

SPECIAL ATTENTION GIVEN TO THE

SETTLEMENT AND COLLECTION OF SOLDIERS' CLAIMS.

OFFICE NEAR THE DEPOT,

MIDDLEPORT, IROQUOIS COUNTY, ILLINOIS.

CHILDS' ENGRAVING ROOMS

117½ RANDOLPH ST.,—First Floor.

LEVER PRESSES AND SEALS FOR STATES,

Counties, Cities, Towns, Courts, Corporations, Notaries and Commissioners, executed in the best style in plain letter, or the most elaborate design,

AT NEW YORK PRICES!

ADDRESS, S. D. CHILDS, JR.,

P. O. Box 83. CHICAGO.

PENSION AND BOUNTY

BLANKS

OF EVERY DESCRIPTION, FOR SALE AT

TRIBUNE OFFICE,

51 Clark Street, Chicago, Ill.

Price, 75 Cents per quire. Sent by mail, post paid, upon receipt of money. Address, personally,

WM. H. RAND, Tribune Office.

DENTISTRY!

W. W. ALLPORT, D. D. S.,

Office & Residence, No. 32 Washington St.

CHICAGO, ILL.

Surgical Operation performed upon the Jaws, and Artificial Jaws and Teeth Inserted.

Pensions, Bounty Money, Arrears of Pay, and Claims against the Government.

WAR CLAIM OFFICE

OF

LEAVITT & WRIGHT,

ATTORNEYS AT LAW,

No. 63 South Clark St., corner Randolph, Chicago.

(Opposite the Sherman House.)

Being the oldest established War Claim Office in Chicago, and having had much experience in prosecuting claims against the Government, special attention is given to obtaining and collecting

PENSIONS due invalid soldiers, the widow and minor heirs of deceased Soldiers.

BOUNTY MONEY AND PAY due the heirs of deceased officers and soldiers.

BACK PAY due resigned officers and discharged soldiers, and all other claims arising out of the present war.

DISCHARGED SOLDIERS sending us their discharge papers, *will receive their pay by return mail.*

NO FEES CHARGED unless the claim is collected.

PATENTS OBTAINED, and Infringement Cases attended to.

☞ *Agents and Correspondents wanted* in every town in the North-West, to whom blanks and instructions will be furnished *gratis*, and a liberal commission allowed.

☞ All kinds of LAW AND COLLECTING business promptly attended to.

Applications received by mail, and any information will be cheerfully given, by addressing

LEAVITT & WRIGHT,

Box 4015, Chicago, Illinois.

FARWELL & CO.

General Commission Merchants!

139 S. WATER STREET, CHICAGO.

LIBERAL ADVANCES MADE ON PROPERTY IN STORE.

CHAS. B. FARWELL. SIMEON FARWELL.

FARWELL'S

STEAM BAG MANUFACTORY

139 SOUTH WATER STREET, CHICAGO.

Bags and Sacks of every variety and description furnished on short notice, and printed with appropriate Brands.

☞BAGS PRINTED IN COLORS.☜

SIMEON FARWELL.

BRIGGS HOUSE

Corner Randolph and Wells Streets,

CHICAGO, - - - - - - - - - - ILLINOIS.

WM. F. TUCKER & CO., Proprietors.

GEORGE S. THOMPSON,

(Late of Commissary General's Office.)

ATTORNEY FOR UNITED STATES MILITARY CLAIMS!

West Side of Public Square,

Entrance Office one door north of Banking House of Messrs. N. H. Ridgely & Co. } **SPRINGFIELD, ILL.**

Having had much experience in presenting claims against the United States, particular attention is given to Recruiting Bills made by Officers and Men of Volunteer Companies and Regiments, for subsisting, collecting, organizing and transporting troops prior to muster into service.

☞ BACK PAY DUE RESIGNED OFFICERS; BACK PAY DUE DISCHARGED SOLDIERS; PAY DUE DECEASED OFFICERS,—THEIR WIDOWS OR HEIRS; BOUNTY AND PAY DUE HEIRS OF DECEASED SOLDIERS; PENSIONS DUE DECEASED SOLDIERS' WIDOWS AND MINOR HEIRS; PENSIONS DUE INVALID SOLDIERS; PAY FOR HORSES LOST, KILLED OR DIED IN THE UNITED STATES SERVICE; ALL CLAIMS GROWING OUT OF THE PRESENT WAR; PENSIONS SEMI-ANNUALLY COLLECTED FROM PENSION AGENT.

Would refer to Messrs. J. WILLIAMS & Co., Bankers, Springfield, Ill.; J. BUNN, Esq., Banker, Sprindfield, Ill.; JOHN BUNN, Esq., Pension Agent, Springfield, Ill.; Capt. C. B. WATSON, U. S. Mustering Officer, Springfield, Ill.

May 20, 1862.

Pension and Bounty Head Quarters!

COL. JAMES W. BOYDEN,

TELEGRAPH BUILDING,

CORNER OF LAKE AND CLARK STS.,

CHICAGO, - - - - - - - - - - ILLINOIS.

COL. BOYDEN'S EXTENSIVE ARRANGEMENTS OFFER UNSURPASSED FACILITIES FOR OBTAINING PAY, PENSIONS, BOUNTY AND OTHER WAR CLAIMS AGAINST THE GOVERNMENT.

PENSIONS.

Pensions for life secured to all persons disabled by wounds, or by disease contracted in the line of duty, and continued, after the Pensioner's death, to his widow or minor children, or dependant mother or orphan sister.

PAY AND BOUNTY.

Pay promptly collected, and one hundred dollars Bounty for the widows and heirs of all who have been killed, or have died of disease contracted in the service.

HOMESTEADS.

The provisions of the new Homestead Bill are expressly extended to all who are in the military and naval service.

APPLICATIONS.

Blank forms furnished and filled at Head Quarters, and by Col. Boyden's Post, Camp and Hospital Agents.

No charge for information, or for correspondence with letter stamp enclosed, or for services, unless successful.

Applications should be made as early as possible, that the papers may be filed at Washington.

Money remitted to claimants, the same day it is received.

Liberal compensation to Agents who are well recommended. Circulars forwarded.

REFERENCES:

For the protection of claimants, they are respectfully referred to the following persons, who will vouch for the integrity, reliability and responsibility of this Agency:

Col. R. Fowler, Cairo,
Dr. Franklin, Mound City Hospital.
Col. Noble, Post Commander, Paducah,
Hon. Ezra Butler, Madison, Ind.
Mayor Bennison, Quincy, Ill.
Rev. W. W. Patton, Chicago Sanitary Commission.
Col. J. W. Foster, " " "
Secretary Seelye, " " "
Chaplain Porter, Sanitary Boat 'Polar Star.'
A. B. Safford, Cashier of Bank, Cairo.
Hon. James H. Woodworth, Prest. Western Marine and Fire Insurance Co., Chicago.
Thomas B. Bryan, Esq., Chicago.
L. J. Gage, Cashier Merchants' Loan and Trust Co., Chicago.
Brig. Quartermaster Howland, in Gen. Paine's Div.
Major General Banks.
Brigadier General Devens.
Cols. Clark and Lee.
Lieut. Col. Guppy, Wisconsin Vol.
Capt. Kennicott, Illinois Vol.
Capt. Waterhouse, of Waterhouse's Ill. Battery.
Lieuts. Chandler and Fitch, " "
Lieut. Hart, Barrett's (late Taylor's) Battery.
Capt. Rounds, Mich. Vol.
Chaplains Anderson, Ill. Vol., and Fisk, Minn. Vol.
Lieuts. Gilman and Jones, Ill. Vol,
Lieut. Lamson, Commanding Gunboat 'Kittaniny,' near New Orleans.
Surgeons Woodworth, Gen. Paine's Div.; Hollister, Camp Douglas; Cheney, Rauch and White, Chicago; Dr. Knowles, Keokuk, Iowa.
Chief Clerk Faxon, Navy Department.
Chief Clerk R. H. Morris, U. S. House Rep.
Hon. Messrs. Arnold, Delano, Dawes and Train, Members of Congress, Washington.

Address, COL. J. W. BOYDEN,

Law, Pension and Bounty Head Quarters,

P. O. Box, 3052, Chicago, Ill.

ISAAC R. HITT & CO.

ATTORNEYS FOR CLAIMANTS,

PENSION, BOUNTY LAND AND PATENT AGENTS

No. 88 DEARBORN ST., CHICAGO, ILL.

Having had *ten* years' experience as Attorneys, prosecuting and adjusting claims of all kinds against the several departments of the Government, we will continue to offer our services in behalf of all claimants who may favor us with a call.

$100 bounty obtained for all soldiers of the present war.

Particular attention given to pensions due officers, soldiers and seamen of the army and navy of the United States, their widows and children.

Claims for indemnity, horses lost or killed, and for the bounty arrears of pay and prize money due officers, soldiers and seamen, or their heirs at law.

Revolutionary, Naval, invalid and half-pay pensions and bounty land procured for those entitled. Claims of military and naval officers, sutlers, contractors, &c., attended to before the proper departments.

Land warrants bought and sold.

Old land patents and land claims purchased, and titles investigated and prosecuted. Patents procured for inventors.

Claims before the General Land Office, under the Preëmption, Swamp Land and Graduation acts. Land Patents. Duplicate Patents and Exemplification of the Records and Files obtained.

We would solicit a correspondence with the *Officers* and *Soldiers* and *Attorneys* of the Northwest, and where our services are required. Except where a special agreement is made, our fee will be contingent upon success.

Hon. John Wilson, formerly Commissioner of the G. L. O., and Samuel T. Shugert, formerly Chief Clerk of the Patent Office for many years, will assist us in all troublesome or intricate cases, at Washington.

Address,

ISAAC R. HITT & CO.,

Chicago, Illinois.

WILLIS M. HITT,

PENSION AND BOUNTY AGENT,

At LA SALLE, ILLINOIS.

☞ **Will attend promptly to any business above specified, addressed to him there.**

SANGER & WHITMORE,

PENSION & BOUNTY LAND AGENTS

AT OTTAWA, ILLINOIS.

☞ **Will attend promptly to any business above specified, addressed to them there.** ☜

NEW YORK CENTRAL
RAILROAD.

GREAT EASTERN DOUBLE TRACK ROUTE.

CONNECTS WITH TRAINS LEAVING CHICAGO, VIA

MICHIGAN CENTRAL RAILROAD
MICHIGAN SOUTHERN R. R.
—AND—
LAKE SHORE LINE via CRESTLINE

FOR ALBANY, TROY,

NEW YORK AND BOSTON.

5 TRAINS LEAVE BUFFALO AND SUSPENSION BRIDGE **DAILY**

☞This is the ONLY ROUTE by which Passengers leaving Chicago Friday Evening, can arrive in New York on Sunday Morning.

Boston Passengers via this Route, save from 14 to 24 hours.

Salsbury's Patent Petticoat Dusters will be attached to all day trains the ensuing season, which deaden the noise so as to render conversation in the cars pleasant and easy, and obviate entirely the inconvenience from dust.

☞SLEEPING CARS☜

Of a pattern acknowledged to be the most Elegant and Comfortable now in use in this Country, will be attached to each Night Train.

ELEGANT SMOKING CARS ATTACHED TO EACH DAY TRAIN.

Baggage Checked Through to N. York and Boston and the principal Towns in New England

FARE ALWAYS AS LOW AS BY ANY OTHER ROUTE.

THROUGH TICKETS Can be procured at all the principal Offices in the West, and at the **Company's Office,** **53 CLARK STREET,** Opposite Sherman House, Chicago.

ALLEN BUTLER, Gen'l Pass. Agent. **JOHN S. CORNING,** Western Ag't, Chicago

MICHIGAN SOUTHERN

AND

LAKE SHORE RAILROAD LINE,

FORMING, WITH ITS CONNECTIONS,

The Great Through Route

Via Cleveland, Dunkirk, or Buffalo, to all Principal Points in

OHIO, PENNSYLVANIA, NEW YORK,

The New England States and Canadas.

TRAINS RUN THROUGH TO DETROIT WITHOUT CHANGE,

MAKING CLOSE

Connections with trains on Gt. Western & Grand Trunk Railways

ALSO, CONNECTING AT CLYDE AND MONROEVILLE WITH TRAINS FOR ALL POINTS IN SOUTHERN OHIO, AND AT CLEVELAND WITH TRAINS

FOR PITTSBURG, HARRISBURG, WHEELING,

BALTIMORE, WASHINGTON, PHILADELPHIA

AND NEW YORK.

SALISBURY'S PATENT DUSTERS ARE USED!

ON ALL DAY TRAINS.

WOODBURY'S PATENT SLEEPING PALACES

ACCOMPANY ALL NIGHT TRAINS.

TICKETS can be procured at all principal Railroad Offices in the West, and at the Company's Office, No. 56 Clark Street, under the Sherman House, and at the Depot, Cor. VanBuren and Sherman Sts.

JNO. D. CAMPBELL,
GEN'L SUPERINTENDENT.

H. E. SAWYER,
GEN'L PASSENGER AGENT.

A. H. MILLER,

IMPORTER, MANUFACTURER & DEALER IN

WATCHES, JEWELRY,

Diamonds, Silver Ware, Spectacles, Clocks, etc.,

126 LAKE STREET, COR. CLARK, CHICAGO.

SPLENDID SWORDS

FOR PRESENTATION, AND FOR MILITARY OFFICERS,

MADE TO ORDER, ORNAMENTED & ENGRAVED

EQUAL TO THOSE OF THE BEST NEW YORK HOUSES.

Fine Watches and Jewelry carefully Repaired on the shortest Notice. All kinds of Jewelry and Silver Ware Made to Order.

NOTICE.—Having greatly enlarged and remodeled the store that I have so long occupied, I shall at all times aim to keep the

Most Extensive and Complete Stock of Jewelry

In Chicago or the North-west, and my aim and endeavor will be to sell just such goods as are represented, so that those entirely unacquainted with the value of Jewelry, will be dealt with fairly.

A. H. MILLER.

THE CHICAGO AND MILWAUKEE

RAILROAD LINE.

THE SHORTEST AND MOST DIRECT ALL RAIL ROUTE TO AND FROM

MILWAUKEE, LACROSSE,

SAINT PAUL,

And all points in Northern Wisconsin, Minnesota and the Northwest generally.

2 EXPRESS PASSENGER TRAINS LEAVE CHICAGO DAILY upon the arrival of Trains from the East, for the accommodation of Travellers going North and Northwest.

TWO TRAINS, ALSO, LEAVE MILWAUKEE DAILY, upon the arrival of Trains from the West, arriving at Chicago on time to make connection with Trains going East and South.

Passengers by this Route avoid the dangers and delay of Navigation of Lake Michigan.

FARE AS LOW AS BY ANY OTHER RAILROAD.

Particular attention paid to the accommodation of Travellers, the handling and safe delivery of Freight.

JNO. T. MOODY,
Master Transportation,
Milwaukee, Wis.

S. C. BALDWIN,
Superintendent,
Chicago, Illinois.

FLORENCE SEWING MACHINE CO.

MANUFACTURERS OF THE

Lock, Double-Lock, Knot, Double-Knot,
and Reversible Feed

SEWING MACHINES

Western Office and Salesroom,

124 Lake St.,

CHICAGO.

There is nothing in this age of "inventive genius" so much sought for by the public as a practical "Sewing Machine." We speak of one by which its correct mechanical structure is found actually to take the place of the hand needle and "tired fingers," and by its simplicity of mechanism to be at all times reliable, and easy of comprehension to any and all persons. Such are the machines of the

FLORENCE SEWING MACHINE CO.

Who take pleasure in placing their machines before the public on their *merits* only.

☞ They make *four* different stitches on one and the same machine, all of which make the same stitch on both sides of the fabric, and can be produced while the machine is in motion.

☞ They have the reversible *feed motion*, which enables the operator to have the work go either way.

☞ *Its motions are all positive*, there are no springs to get out of order, and so simplified that the most inexperienced can work it perfectly with ease.

☞ *It is a noiseless machine*, and can be used where quiet is necessary, in the sick chamber as well as in the work room.

☞ *It is the most rapid sewer in the world;* makes five stitches to each revolution.

☞ *It does the heaviest or finest work;* both with equal facility and without change of machinery or tension.

☞ *It is fully protected and licensed* under the patents of Elias Howe, Jr., and his associates, and under our own letters patent.

Any correspondence or orders will be promptly attended to if addressed to

W. C. MASON, Agent.

www.ingramcontent.com/pod-product-compliance
Lightning Source LLC
La Vergne TN
LVHW021426110826
845150LV00007B/2105
* 9 7 8 1 4 2 5 5 0 7 2 0 6 *